Orders: Please contact How2Become Ltd, Suite 14, 50 Churchill Square Business Centre, Kings Hill, Kent ME19 4YU.

You can order through Amazon.co.uk under ISBN 9781911259879, via the website www.How2Become.com, Gardners or Bertrams.

ISBN: 9781911259879

First published in 2017 by How2Become Ltd.

Typeset for How2Become Ltd by Gemma Butler.

Disclaimer

Every effort has been made to ensure that the information contained within this guide is accurate at the time of publication. How2Become Ltd is not responsible for anyone failing any part of any selection process as a result of the information contained within this guide. How2Become Ltd and their authors cannot accept any responsibility for any errors or omissions within this guide, however caused. No responsibility for loss or damage occasioned by any person acting, or refraining from action, as a result of the material in this publication can be accepted by How2Become Ltd.

The information within this guide does not represent the views of any third-party service or organisation.

Contents

INTRODUCTION

Welcome to *How to Get a First at University.* In this book, you will learn expert tips and gain insightful advice on how to finish your university course with a first-class degree.

Getting a first at university might seem incredibly challenging, and in many ways, it is. You have to be committed to your studies throughout your course, and often go the extra mile to get those extra marks.

So, in this book, you'll learn expert advice in the following areas to improve your chances of getting a first-class degree:

- How to plan your degree;
- Study techniques and learning styles;
- How to ace your coursework;
- How to plan and complete your dissertation or project;
- How to prepare for revision;
- Exam techniques;
- How to handle stress.

Before continuing, we need to answer the basics.

What Is a First-Class Degree?

A first-class honours degree, or a 'first', is the highest class of degree you can get at undergraduate level. For this reason, it's incredibly sought after by the keenest students, and is looked upon favourably by employers across all kinds of industries and fields.

Generally speaking, a first is awarded to students who achieve an average of at least 70% in their university course. This means that, when the average is calculated across every formal piece of work you've handed in, including coursework, projects, and exams, the mean score must be at least 70%.

The work that counts toward your final score at the end of your degree is sometimes referred to as *summative*, whilst work that is graded but **does not** contribute to your degree is *formative*. This means that, as a rule, your summative work should take priority over formative work. Bear in mind that this terminology might differ depending on your university. However, in most cases, the marks you gain for work in your first year will not count towards your degree score, but that in your second year and beyond will.

If you aren't sure what work will count towards your final score, you should ask departmental staff such as secretaries, lecturers, or tutors.

Why Does It Matter?

Having a first-class degree puts you ahead of your competition when it comes to the job market. While many employers expect an upper second-class degree (a '2:1') or higher for graduate schemes rather than a first, having a first will give you an advantage over those who have met the minimum requirement.

In 2014, the Higher Education Statistics Agency found that approximately 20% of students in the UK achieved a first-class degree. This means that having a first would potentially place you in the top 20% of students in your year, making you a great catch for employers. For this reason alone, it's well worth putting in the time to get a first.

Aside from that, getting a first-class degree demonstrates a commitment to your studies on your part, and is something to be proud of. While you should take pride in any degree you end up with, a first shows commitment, intelligence, and a strong work ethic. In short, possessing a first-class degree indicates excellence on your part.

Finally, the road to getting a first-class degree is a rewarding one. In order to do it, you'll need to work hard, learn a lot about your subject, and also acquire skills in how to study and retain information, how to write or manage a project, and how to effectively handle stress and a work-life balance. Most of these are vital skills in the workplace and everyday life, and all of them are preferable. Having a first-class degree is more than just a certificate or a grade – it's evidence of how much you've achieved, as well as the skills you've gained along the way.

How Is Degree Level Different to GCSE and A-Level?

Degree level is almost completely different to GCSE and A-Level. The style and structure of teaching is incredibly different, the amount of independent study required is much greater, the level of understanding and the style of working are leagues apart from what was expected at school, and the resources available are much greater. Essentially, university is almost entirely different to GCSE and A-Level in every way.

However, this doesn't mean that you can't take what you've learned at GCSE and A-Level and apply them to your university studies. At the end of Chapter 3, we'll discuss how you can learn from your earlier studies to maximise your efficiency at degree level.

As previously mentioned, however, university is different to GCSE and A-Level in a lot of ways. The differences between university and your studies at school range from the way courses are taught, all the way up to how you write and submit your work.

Firstly, university courses are taught in a very different way to GCSE and A-Level. At school, you likely had multiple lessons a day, back-to-back, in classes of up to thirty students. The relatively low number probably meant that your teachers could know you quite well. In turn, this could have allowed them to keep an eye on your progress, and steer you in the right direction so that you could get the grades you wanted

At university, this is often not the case. Generally speaking, university courses contain two different types of teaching sessions – lectures and seminars (sometimes referred to as 'tutorials'). The likelihood is that you will have both at university, although some courses might opt for one or the other exclusively.

Lectures are regular teaching sessions, and usually take place in larger lecture halls in the university buildings. This is because lectures hold a lot of students in them – every student taking the module will be housed in the same room for the lecture. This means that, for more popular modules in the most subscribed courses, lectures might contain up over a hundred students – a massive increase on the number found in most school classes.

What this means for students is that lecturers won't be able to give individual attention to students. Instead, they focus on presenting the core information required to complete the assessments of the module. Generally speaking, this is delivered in the form of presentations on a projector. Bear in mind that what you learn in lectures is usually the **bare minimum** for passing the module. In order to do well, you'll also need to prepare for seminars.

Seminars are the secondary point of learning for university students. These sessions are sometimes less frequent than lectures (often fortnightly as opposed to weekly), although this can differ depending on your university, course, and module. Seminar groups tend to be much smaller in number than lectures, which means that you'll have a greater chance for one-to-one time with your seminar leader. This means that they can keep track of you more than a lecturer can. Seminars are where you'll be doing supplementary work and discussions; you'll often have to prepare for them either by completing assignments, preparing for group work or doing additional reading.

While seminar groups are smaller, and seminar leaders might be able to give more individual attention to you, it's worth remembering that the vast majority of university courses focus on individual study. This means that you shouldn't expect to be spoon-fed information and coast through your degree. University is designed specifically for students to spend time studying independently.

This change from class-based work to independent learning is probably the toughest for most students to get used to. Mastery of this is the key to success at degree level. So, in Chapter 3, we'll be taking a look at how to study independently.

Achieving a First

A first-class degree is reserved for the most committed students with the most exemplary work. Therefore, getting a first can be a challenge for a lot of students. This doesn't mean that they are unattainable, however.

In most degrees, a first is awarded to students who get an average of at least 70% across all of their assessed work. Here's a chart of all the different classes of degree you can get, and what the average required mark is for each:

Level	Required Score (Average)
Third-Class ('Third')	40%
Lower Second-Class ('2:2')	50%
Upper Second-Class ('2:1')	60%
First-Class ('First')	70%

If you've been getting As and A*s at A-Level, then achieving a first might look easy. After all, you need 80% at A-Level to get an A, so getting 70% at university seems to be easier.

However, this isn't the case at all. University work is marked to a much higher standard than A-Levels, and so getting those top scores is much more challenging. Make no mistake – getting a first isn't easy. However, it's absolutely within your grasp if you take the time to study and prepare.

Who Is This Book For?

This book is written with the following kinds of people in mind:

- Students who are currently planning on going to university, and want some guidance on how to perform as well as possible prior to starting their degree;

- Students beginning their journey at university, wanting to get ahead of the curve and prepare to get a first;

- Students who are part way through their degree, and want to get some extra tips to boost their studies and increase their chances of success.

So, whether you're yet to go to university, just starting, or well on your way to completing your degree, this book will cater to you. While this book is written with those attempting to get a first in mind, anyone at university level can make use of the content in this guide. Whether you're expecting a first, 2:1, 2:2, or a third, the advice given in this book will be useful for you.

What Areas Will This Book Cover?

In this guide, we'll be taking a look at the entire degree process. Here's a summary of each chapter:

- **Planning Your Degree** – Here, we'll discuss the first steps of getting yourself onto a course that suits you, and how to prepare to get excellent grades from the very beginning. This is a recommended chapter for students who are just starting their degree, or are preparing to go to university;

- **How to Study Independently** – As previously mentioned, independent study is vital for success at university. In this chapter, you'll learn the top tips for nailing independent study and improving your chances of success;

- **General Study Techniques** – In this chapter, you'll learn about different methods for revision and studying. First, you'll have the opportunity to find out what learning style suits you. Then, study techniques that are suitable for your learning style will be detailed, giving you some ideas on how to revise effectively;

- **Acing Coursework** – Here, we'll go into detail on ongoing assessments at university, and how to be consistent when it comes to achieving great grades;

- **Getting Started with Your Revision** – This chapter will discuss how to get started with revision, from how to motivate yourself, all the way up to making a timetable and sticking to it;

- **Exam Techniques and Preparation** – In this final chapter, we'll be focusing on how to perform well in your exams.

You can either read this book from start to finish, or dip into the chapters which you find most relevant. Each chapter is designed to be read independently of the others. However, you will get the most out of this book if you read it in chronological order.

PLANNING YOUR DEGREE

Now that we've taken an overall look at the contents of this book, it's time to consider how to plan your degree so that you're best prepared to get the highest marks possible.

In this chapter, we're going to be looking at the following three key areas:

- Choosing your course – how to choose a university course that will serve your future goals, and give you the best chance of getting a first;

- Choosing your modules – how to pick the modules and topics which will make getting a first as straightforward as possible;

- Creating an assessment timetable – a guide to getting all of the key dates for your course in order, so you're never caught out by a deadline and have plenty of time to complete your work.

The first section of this chapter will only apply to those who haven't chosen their degree yet. So, if you're already studying at university, skip to the second section on choosing modules.

Choosing Your Course

The first step to starting your degree and getting a first is choosing the course that you want to do. Universities offer a huge range of different subjects – so many that we can't list them all here. Whatever you're interested in, there's almost certainly a subject which applies to you.

While some courses might be 'easier' to get a first in than others, this isn't a good reason to choose a subject at university. First and foremost, you should choose a course that you're interested in. You'll be spending a minimum of three years studying for your degree – you don't want to waste those years and all that effort doing something you're not interested in.

The second reason for choosing something that you're interested in is because you're more likely to perform well in it. This is because, if you enjoy the subject, you'll be motivated to go the extra mile and learn more. A lot of university courses will require you to do extra reading, research, assessments, and homework outside of lecture and seminar hours, so it's vital that you enjoy what you're studying both for your own sake and for the sake of your grades.

The other factor to consider when choosing your degree is what you want to do in the future. A lot of careers don't require a specific degree in order to start them (some don't require a degree at all), but there are plenty which do. The following are a few careers which require a specific degree:

Career	Required Degree
Doctor	Medicine
Engineer	Engineering
Nurse	Nursing
Vet	Veterinary Science
Dentist	Dentistry
Researcher (Science)	Degree in the area of science that you want to go into (e.g. Physics)
Lawyer	Law Qualification

While a lot of jobs don't require a specific degree, many will expect degrees from a certain area. For example, if you want to become a copywriter, you'll probably be expected to have a background in writing. So, degrees which focus heavily on essay writing, such as English Literature, Philosophy, and Law, will be favourable.

If you currently have an idea about what type of career you'd like to go into, try and find some job listings online and see what kind of degrees the employers are looking for. Then, if you're passionate about a specific career, you can find a degree which will give you the best chance of getting there.

If you don't know what career you want, don't worry! You have plenty of time to decide, and even if you end up wanting to go down a path which requires specific qualifications, there are postgraduate opportunities to do so. Focus on doing something that you love first, then see where it can take you.

The final thing to consider when looking at university courses is what kind of assessment they use. For example, some subjects focus heavily on exams as a form of assessment. Courses such as Maths will be mostly exam-based, so if you know that you struggle with exams it might not be such a good idea to study Maths. Likewise, if you know that coursework and constant assessment gives you a hard time, then a subject which focuses on lots of exams at the end of the year might be a better choice for you.

The way a course is made up and assessed will depend from university to university. See how different institutions have constructed their courses and then see which one suits you the best. Try and find a structure that will best suit your style of learning and working.

Choosing Your Modules

Let's skip forward a year or two now and assume that you're at university. Either you've just started your degree, or you're a year or two in. Usually, students at university have at least some choice in which modules they take. You'll be given a list of available modules before the start of the new academic year, and you'll have to choose between them.

This can be a difficult decision to make, but we recommend that you choose modules in a similar way to how we suggested that you choose your choice. Consider the following questions:

1. Does the content of the module interest me, and will I find it enjoyable enough to go the extra mile and do more work?

2. Is the teaching structure more lecture-based or seminar-focused?

3. What is the assessment structure of the module like? Is it more coursework-based or exam-focused?

4. Is assessment constant throughout the year, or do I write and submit everything at the very end?

5. Are there any unusual elements to the module, such as practical lab work, field trips, or anything else that I might enjoy

or struggle with?

6. Do I need to take specific modules *this year* to access modules in later years?

7. Can I find out more information about the module on the university website so that I know I want to take it?

8. What is the quality of teaching like in the module?

9. What do students in previous years have to say about the module?

10. How long does the module last for?

Let's take a look at each of these questions in a bit more detail:

Does the content of the module interest me, and will I find it enjoyable enough to go the extra mile and do more work?
As we said in the previous section, enjoyment should be your priority when choosing a module. Most university departments will have their own website – modules should be detailed there. Find a breakdown of the module's content and see what the areas of study are before picking it. This is important because if you enjoy the module, you're probably going to perform better in it than one that you either hate or don't care about.

Is the teaching structure more lecture-based or seminar-focused?
This will be important to you when creating a study timetable. It's also important to find out what is expected of you during these sessions. For example, seminars might require that you do some extra reading, create a presentation, work with others, or complete a homework exercise. If possible, find out if a module includes these before you choose it.

What is the assessment structure of the module like? Is it more coursework-based or exam-focused?
As previously mentioned, some courses and modules will be more focused on one style of assessment or another. Some modules might only have coursework and others might only feature exams. You'll

find that a lot of modules will make use of both, with coursework assessment to be found throughout the year and exams at the very end of it.

It's also important to find out how much of the assessed work counts towards your final grade. For example, a module might require that you write three essays, but only two of those are summative. This means that only two of them will count towards your final grade. If this is the case, you can prioritise the work which will have the biggest impact on your degree.

Finally, find out what the ratio of marks between the different assessments is. For example, a module might be weighted so that 60% of the marks are available in coursework, whilst 40% is available in the final exam. If the coursework is made up of two essays of equal value, then you know that each essay is worth 30% of the module. You can use this to plan out your work and make sure that you secure as many marks as possible.

Is assessment constant throughout the year, or do I write and submit everything at the very end?
This will be important to you if you have a particular style of working. If you have constant assessment throughout the year, then you'll be forced to work constantly in order to keep to deadlines. In contrast, having all of your work to do at the very end of the year could make you complacent until the final weeks, which could put you in a lot of trouble. Think about how you've dealt with assessment, revision, and studying in the past and how that relates to the assessment structure of a module.

Are there any unusual elements to the module, such as practical lab work, field trips, or anything else that I might enjoy or struggle with?
This will depend on the course you are taking. Generally speaking, courses in the sciences are the only ones which will contain practical work, but others might include trips. In particular, try and find out how much of this is assessed.

Do I need to take specific modules *this year* to access modules in later years?
Sometimes, a department will specify that a module in later years has prerequisite modules. For example, a third-year module that you want to do might require a certain second-year module being taken. Take this into account when picking modules for each year, since your choices might limit your options in later years of your degree.

Can I find out more information about the module on the university website so that I know I want to take it?
In most cases, universities have department websites that list the available modules for each year. This usually includes a breakdown of content, as well as a breakdown of marks. Answers to most of the questions we've looked at here can be found on these department websites, so make sure that you read them carefully before committing to a module.

What is the quality of teaching like in the module?
This is a tricky question to get an answer for because the university is unlikely to admit that a module is being taught poorly, since this would reflect poorly on the institution as a whole. The best way to find out the quality of teaching for a module is to find some older students on your course who are either taking the module right now or have done so in the past. Hopefully, your university has programmes which allow for mentoring from students in the years above your own. This will allow you to hear from students themselves if a module is worth taking or not.

What do students in previous years have to say about the module?
This ties into the previous question about teaching quality, since you'll probably have to speak with other students to get an answer. They might also be able to give you greater insight into what's expected of you, the best places to find additional reading, and how to perform well in your assessments and exams.

How long does the module last for?
This will differ between universities and departments. Whilst many modules will last for the entire year, some may be shorter. Keep this

in mind when choosing a module because, if it does take less than a year to complete, the final assessment for the module could appear earlier in the year. You don't want to get caught out by it!

Finally, remember that you aren't necessarily locked into a module after choosing it. Universities often allow students to change modules during the first term if the individual is unsatisfied with its content. Find out what the policy of your university and department are if you're worried that you might want to change modules.

Creating an Assessment Timetable

Let's assume that you're currently at university, and you've picked your modules for the year. First of all, congratulations – even making it to university is commendable.

From here, you need to start thinking about how you're going to organise your work throughout the year. You've probably got a lot of different modules to study for, and depending on your course this could take all kinds of forms. Prioritising your work and getting ready for the year or term will put you on the right track for achieving a first.

The first thing to do is find out what the assessment structure is for each module that you're taking. Usually, this information can be found on your department website. Take note of how many essays or assignments you have to complete throughout the year, as well as the number of exams you'll be given at the end.

Once you know every piece of work that you have to hand in, you need to find out whether they are assessed as summative work or formative work. Remember, summative assignments count towards your final mark at the end of the year, whilst formative ones do not. For each of the summative assignments, find out how much of the module they are worth. For example, the two essays in a module might make up 40% of the marks in the module overall, whilst the exam is worth 60%. Take note of this since it will let you figure out what you should prioritise.

With the number and value of each assessment in mind, it's time to get the dates of the deadlines. The exact date might not be made available immediately, but department websites should give a rough indication (for example, 'one essay due at the end of the first term').

Universities and departments will handle these deadlines in different ways. Some courses will have a load of assignments across all of your modules due at around the same time at the end of term, whilst others might stagger them slightly so that you don't feel overwhelmed in the final week of term.

If all of your deadlines land at the same time in the final week of term, don't try to do them all in a short space of time. Try to find out the assignment task as early as possible during the term so that you can get started on them as soon as possible.

Take a look at the following table which suggests how you might want to approach assignments during the year. This table assumes that each essay takes one week to complete. Depending on the amount of preparation you need to do for each, and how fast you are at working, this might take more time. Also, bear in mind that you might have more assessments than this, or potentially less.

Week	Essays	Deadlines
1		
2		
3		
4	Essay 1	
5	Essay 2	
6	Essay 3	
7	Essay 4	Essay 1
8	Essay 5	
9	Essay 6	Essay 2 Essay 3
10		Essay 4 Essay 5 Essay 6

Here, you can see how each essay is due well before its deadline. Completing Essay 1 in Week 4 means that it's finished with two weeks spare. This means that, if you need to go back and make some final adjustments, there's plenty of time to do so. This method of spacing out your assessments means that you aren't overworking yourself at the end of term. Make an assignment plan so that each piece of assessed work gets enough attention.

Next, you need to consider which assessments should take priority. Of course, you should try to complete everything to an equal standard. Even if an assessment is formative, submitting it with as much effort put into it as possible will still be helpful for the following reasons:

1. Formative assessments can be used to consolidate your own knowledge on areas you might need for summative assessments or exams later in the year.

2. They're a great form of practice, especially for essay-based modules.

3. You'll likely receive feedback from the person who marked your work, letting you know whether you're on the right track or not.

For these reasons, you should take formative assessments seriously. However, sometimes you'll be faced with a lot of summative work that simply needs to take precedence. If you have to, prioritise the work that directly affects your overall grade at the end of the year. However, this doesn't mean you should ignore formative work – it's also extremely important.

Conclusion

By now, you should be ready to go into the next year or term with the following in mind:

- The course that you're studying;

- The modules that you've picked;

- The style of assessment for each module;

- The details and value of each assessment;

- The approximate deadlines for each assessment;

- The time that you're going to complete each assessment in (approximately).

If you know all of these, and have a timetable ready, then you're well prepared to start the term. Remember that you can always change your timetable if you think you've overestimated or underestimated on how much time things will take, especially if you're in your first term of university. Over time, you'll get a feel for how long it takes for you to complete an assignment, and so you can make a better prediction in your timetable for when it will be finished by. Giving yourself plenty of time to research and complete each assignment is one of the best ways to get a first.

In order to complete these assignments, you'll also need to know how to study independently. This is the focus of the next chapter.

HOW TO STUDY INDEPENDENTLY

At school, you most likely had a lot of guidance from teachers, did most of your work in classrooms with help at hand, and were given most of the reading and work you had to do. You weren't handed everything on a platter, but it's probable that you had a lot of support.

At university, this changes considerably. While you'll have lectures and seminars to guide you on the right path, most of the work will be left to you. On the one hand, this is extremely liberating; outside of these organised sessions, you can work to your own hours. However, there's also a level of responsibility that comes with this, in that you need to be able to work on your own. For this reason, being able to study independently is the single most important skill for anyone at university.

In this chapter, we'll discuss the key ways that you can improve your chances of success at university by learning to study independently. This will include:

- What independent study is;

- How to conduct and gather research with minimal guidance;

- How to make use of a range of resources available to you;

- How to stay focused and motivated.

There's a lot of responsibility on the individual when it comes to independent study. From motivating yourself to get up and work, to having a good understanding of everything at your disposal, by the end of this chapter you'll have a strong idea of how to get yourself ready for independent study.

What is Independent Study?

Before continuing, let's briefly touch on what independent study is. Independent study at university level can be broken up into the following areas:

- Independent research, such as finding books from the library to read for an upcoming seminar;

- Independent homework, such as a Maths workbook filled with problems to solve;

* Independent studying for a piece of coursework, such as an essay or lab report;

* Independent revision for exams.

By independent study, we mean any study that isn't overseen by a teacher, lecturer, or seminar. For many students, independent study will occupy the majority of their time. Others, however, will have less independent work to do.

For example, students studying Maths will generally have a lot of contact hours (lectures and seminars). While they'll have a lot of independent work to do on top of this, they'll generally have less independently study than students taking Humanities degrees.

A student studying History, for example, will have far fewer contact hours. Because of this, these students will be expected to read much more on their own time. While this might not balance out perfectly between Science degrees and Humanities courses, the general rule is that the fewer contact hours you have, the more independent work you'll be expected to do.

Conducting Research Alone

Conducting independent research is useful for any subject, but vital for those studying degrees with fewer contact hours. This is because these students will have a lot more work to do on their own time.

If you're studying one of the Humanities or Social Sciences, then you'll have to do a lot of reading on your own, usually on a daily basis. This could be set reading for a seminar or lecture, or just general reading to get you ahead in your next piece of coursework. Whatever the case, you'll need to be able to work on your own in order to stay ahead of the game and improve your chances of getting a first.

When it comes to almost any module, you'll probably be given a list of sources which will be relevant to you. This tends to consist of the following:

1. **Core sources.** These are usually text books or primary reading, with the suggestion that you should purchase these for yourself since you'll be referring to them often.

2. **Further core texts.** Typically, these are available in the university library, or the lecturer will be printing handouts of specific chapters.

3. **Seminar sources.** These are usually set by your seminar leader, but can also be set by lecturers too. In a lot of cases, these will be made readily available via printed handouts or digital copies, unless they are already easily accessible online.

4. **Further reading.** These sources are usually reserved for students writing about a specific topic within the module. When it comes to completing assignments at the end of term, you'll want to find the further reading that's suitable for your module. If you aren't writing your coursework on this topic, you probably won't have to worry about this until the end of the year when it comes to exam revision.

Try to complete your reading in this order. Start with the 'core' works since they are usually picked for being the best introduction to a module or topic, with the reading becoming more specialised over time.

In addition to these areas, it might be worth looking at companion pieces to core texts. This is particularly useful for Humanities subjects such as English Literature, Philosophy, or History. If you're reading a core text written a long time ago, it might be helpful to read a secondary source which helps you contextualise it. For example, if you're reading *The Odyssey*, it would be handy to have a secondary work that you can read alongside the main text.

This way, you'll be given additional insight into the primary source, which will make understanding it much easier. This won't be relevant for all courses, and not all of your primary texts will have companion pieces. However, this will be incredibly useful for the modules that do.

When it comes to exam season, make use of all of the areas we've spoken about. In addition, you can find lots of revision sources online. Even websites such as YouTube might have appropriate materials for revision. When using these extra sources, make sure that the content is relevant. If you aren't entirely sure if it's suitable, ask your seminar leader or lecturer.

Gathering Research

The first step to success when studying independently is getting hold of the information that you need. There are two major locations that you'll likely get most of your research from:

- The university library/libraries;

- The internet.

On top of this, you might have bought some books yourself. We recommend this for the core reading that you might have for your modules. Everything else that you need should be obtainable from the library or online resources.

We recommend that you get hold of the books you'll need from the library as soon as you know which ones are required. This is because university libraries don't always hold more than one or two copies of the same book, and these can get checked out quickly. Departments and modules usually send out reading lists at the start of the year's first term. Find out exactly what you need and get hold of it as soon as you can.

Once you have these books, try to read them as soon as you can. This is because most university libraries allow for students to recall books that they need. This means that you might have to return a book to the library earlier than you expected. If you haven't read the book yet, you'll likely be in a rush to get all of the notes that you need. Read the essential chapters and take notes on them. Then, if the book gets recalled, you can return it without feeling as though you didn't make the most of it.

Once you've written your notes on the books you've taken out, it's time to get online for everything else. When it comes to set work, your seminar leaders and lecturers might make specific chapters available to you. Make use of these first since they are hand-picked by university staff and therefore will be most relevant to you. Take notes on these after you've finished working on the books you've taken out from the library.

After working on the chapters given by university staff, it's time to head online and get some extra reading. You'll have a hard time finding full books online for free – you'll mainly be sticking to journals and articles. It's quite possible that your university has access to one of the many online journal archives. These are excellent resources since they're free for you to use, and host a wealth of content across all fields. If you do have access to one of these, make full use of them and look up any additional reading suggested by your lecturers. These can be invaluable for adding some extra flair to your work.

Staying Motivated

While it's good to tell you how to make use of the resources at your disposal, and how to work well independently, it's just as important to be able to stay motivated. Here are a few measures you can take to keep yourself motivated and focused:

Turn off Distractions

The first step to a productive studying session is to make sure nothing is going to steal your attention. If you're going to be working at a computer, log out of all of your social media, or at the very least turn notifications off. If you're really struggling to stay away from things such as social media, you can temporarily block the websites on the computer that you're using.

Try and keep your mobile phone away from your workspace while you're working. If you're working in your own private space such as your bedroom, try to keep the phone as far away as possible so it can't distract you at all.

Set up a Rewards System

To keep yourself motivated, set up a system where you give yourself a reward for completing a chunk of work. Divide everything you need to do into sections, then give yourself a reward of some kind once each section is complete.

For example, you might say "if I manage to take notes on the next two chapters, I'll take a break to play video games." This way, you're planning breaks into your timetable, as well as giving yourself a reason to push forward and get the next piece of work finished.

Stick to a Routine
A messy studying schedule can make it incredibly difficult to sit down and work. To avoid this, try to set aside a specific time of day, every day, devote to studying. For some students, it helps to get up relatively early in the morning and treat each day as though it were a regular work or school day – even if they don't have many lectures or seminars to attend.

Attend Your Lectures
This might seem obvious, but a lot of students tend to skip lectures once they know that all of the notes will be available online, or if the topic doesn't interest them. This can be dangerous, because it can lead to complacency. Some students will skip lectures at inconvenient hours, such as early in the morning. You're much better off getting a good night's sleep, waking up in time for your lectures and seminars, and then getting on with the rest of your studies throughout the day.

In addition, an interesting lecture might be what you need to get inspired for getting back to work in your own time. So, it pays to attend them even if you'd rather just stay in bed!

Discuss with Others
In the same sense that a great lecture could inspire you, chatting about your work with fellow students might give you new insights or reinvigorate your desire to learn. If you have friends on your course who are up for it, you could organise weekly or fortnightly meetings where you discuss notes. This could give you the impetus to keep up with your studying.

Conclusion
Now you should have a good idea about how to study independently,

how to make use of the resources at your disposal, as well as how to stay motivated. In the next chapter, we'll be taking a look at general study techniques which can be used for revision, studying for coursework, or any other area that you might be working on.

GENERAL
STUDY
TECHNIQUES

Why Should I Revise?

You might have heard the phrase 'failing to prepare is preparing to fail', basically stating that people who do not revise should expect to perform poorly. While this isn't universally the case – some people 'wing it' and manage to do brilliantly in exams – it holds true in most circumstances. Preparation is possibly the most influential factor in your exam performance. No matter how smart you are, preparation will unlock your true potential and allow you to get the best marks possible.

In the past, you might've got away with coasting through exams. While this is certainly more relaxing, it incurs a lot of risk. If you're serious about the opportunities that passing your exams will bring, you'll take the time to prepare. For example, if you're planning on becoming a train driver, there are numerous tests you'll have to sit. If you're passionate about your goals and want to achieve them, you'll take the preparation and revision processes very seriously indeed.

As we'll see in this book, preparation takes several forms outside of revision. It also involves maintaining a healthy diet and a good sleep regime. In addition, any respectable preparation will also involve writing and sticking to a revision timetable. All of these – and more – will need to be taken into account. This can seem like a lot at first, but that's exactly what this guide is for.

The Three Styles of Learning

There are three major ways that people revise and absorb information. These are:

*   **Visual** – This involves using visual aids such as note-taking and creative mapping of information, to commit things to memory.

*   **Aural** – The use of videos, music or other recordings to allow information to sink in.

*   **Kinaesthetic** – Using activities which involve interaction, to remember key details (such as flashcards and revision games).

Different paths will work better for different people, but also bear in mind that certain subjects will also suit these methods differently. For example, Maths may be better suited to visual learning than aural learning, because mathematics (sums and equations) is more visually-oriented than other subjects. However, certain rules or formulae could be learned by placing notes around your study space, if you're a kinaesthetic learner.

Essentially, you will need to experiment with different styles in order to find which best suits you, but you will also need to discover which works for each of your subjects. In the next three sections, we will examine the different methods of learning in more detail. Additionally, each method will be paired with the subjects which best suit it, as well as how to identify which style matches your own.

The quickest way to figure out what kind of learner you are, is to think of what works best for you when trying to remember something. When someone needs to explain to you how to do something, what sinks in the best? Do you learn by watching others doing it first, or by listening to their explanation? Alternatively, you might learn best by giving it a try yourself. Use the following quick guide to figure out what kind of learner you might be:

- **Visual** – You learn best by watching others or reading information. If you're learning a technique in a game, sport, or other activity, you would prefer to watch videos of others doing it, watching people do it in real life, or by reading explanations. You might also learn from looking at images or diagrams.

- **Aural** – Listening is your preferred style of learning. You would rather ask for and listen to directions rather than look at a map. If you were learning something new, you'd rather listen to an explanation and follow the instructions.

- **Kinaesthetic** – You learn by doing things rather than just listening or reading. Rather than being told how to do something, you try to do it yourself. You prefer practical, energetic ways of learning as opposed to the traditional methods of reading, listening and note-taking.

Learning Style Quiz

The following learning style quiz can be used to figure out which of the above learning styles suits you best. Once you're done, head to the answers section, where all will be revealed!

1. If you were watching an advertisement for a product on TV, how would you most likely react?

A) You'd notice the imagery, colours and other things happening on screen.

B) You'd recognise and listen to the music, and maybe even hum along if you knew it well enough.

C) You'd remember a time when you saw or interacted with the product in real life.

2. You're using a programme on your computer and can't figure out how to perform a specific task. How would you learn how to do it?

A) Watch an online video tutorial of someone doing it.

B) Ask someone to tell you how to do it.

C) Attempt it yourself until you figure out how it's done.

3. If you had to learn lines for a theatre production, how would you do it?

A) Sit down with the script and read your lines in your head.

B) Read the lines out loud to yourself.

C) Get together with a few other people and act out your scene(s).

4. You need to remember someone's postcode, so that you can find their house. How do you best remember it?

A) Visualise the letters and numbers.

B) Repeat the postcode out loud to yourself.

C) Write it down.

5. You're doing some fairly simple mental arithmetic. How would you solve the sum?

A) By visualising it in your head.

B) By saying the numbers and the operation out loud, step by step.

C) By counting or subtracting on your fingers, or by using objects nearby (such as counting pens and pencils).

6. Which of the following would you most likely do for fun?

A) Watch TV.

B) Listen to a radio show or podcast.

C) Play a video game.

7. You're queueing for a theme park ride and the wait time is quite long. Which of the following would you most notice whilst in the queue?

A) The decorations in the queueing areas.

B) The music or sound effects playing in the background.

C) How long it's been since you last moved in the queue.

8. If you saw the word "apple" written down, how would you react?

A) By visualising the word "apple" in your head.

B) By saying the word out loud to yourself.

C) By imagining things related to apples (cores, pips, trees, etc).

9. You're in a new place for the first time and need directions. What would you do?

A) Find a map and follow it.

B) Ask someone for directions.

C) Keep walking around until you find the location for yourself.

10. When you meet a new person, what do you remember the most?

A) Their face.

B) Their name.

C) What you did with them, or what you talked about.

Now that you've finished, you can find out what kind of learner you are:

- **If most of your answers were A**, then you are a visual learner. You learn by using your eyes to analyse diagrams and notes.

- **If most of your answers were B**, then you are an aural learner. Spoken words sink in best, so you do well when listening to yourself or others.

- **If most of your answers were C**, then you are a kinaesthetic learner. You study best when getting involved and doing things for yourself, rather than watching or listening.

Remember that you don't necessarily have to fall into just one of these three categories. A wide range of learning methods might work for you, so it's good to keep experimenting to find out which techniques suit you best.

In the next few sections, we will cover the three main styles of learning, so you can get some top tips on how to study efficiently!

Visual Learning

Visual learning is exactly as it sounds – you learn by visually representing information, or by having information visually represented for you. This can involve pages of notes, mind maps, tables, animations, slideshows and more. All of these can be used to make information easy to digest visually.

While modern computers are adept at note-taking and mind map making, you might find it more helpful to ditch the laptop for a while and use a pen and paper. This way, you can improve your handwriting skills, make notes which are available at any time, as well as avoid distractions which come too easily whilst on a computer connected to the internet!

Visual learning is excellent for any subject that has a lot of written text to digest, where a passage of information needs to be dissected to find the most important parts. Note-taking can condense a whole chapter of dates, facts and figures into a page or two. Mind maps are a great way of connecting many key facts to a single core concept, such as an event or an important person. Additionally, videos and slideshows are excellent for representing data in a clear manner.

Visual learners tend to be good at remembering images and charts. They'll likely find it easier to remember details of pictures and photographs, and might perform well in memory games where they have to spot which object has been removed from a collection. For this reason, visual learners are suited to organising their revision materials into diagrams, which they will likely find easy to remember.

Depending on what you're studying for, you'll have a huge amount of information that you need to retain for the exams. Some of the following visual learning techniques, such as note-taking and mind maps, are excellent for holding onto large amounts of facts.

Note-taking and Summarisation

This method is exactly as it sounds: you write down notes based on the information in your textbooks or lesson materials. The goal is to collect all of the vital information from your resources. Use the following steps to take notes effectively:

1. Read through your textbook and other learning materials once, without making notes. Do this so that you get an overall understanding of the material.

2. Go back to the start of the material and begin to re-write the key details in your own words. Alternatively, if the book belongs to you, you can underline key points.

3. Continue re-writing important details until you've finished a whole chapter. Make sure to organise the bullet points into sections.

4. Once finished, read over your notes.

5. Then, turn your pages of notes over so you can't see them, then try to remember as much as possible.

6. Repeat this until you're able to remember all of your notes

without reading them.

How you go about writing these notes will depend on what you're studying and which techniques best suit you. One way to help notes stick in your head is to underline the key words from sentences in your text books or other materials. Once you've done that, you can lay them out in your notes. This is beneficial because it separates the important details from the less important ones. For example:

> *"One of the <u>key themes</u> of William Shakespeare's 'Othello' is <u>jealousy</u>. <u>Iago warns Othello</u> of jealousy being a <u>"green-eyed monster,"</u> and ultimately <u>it's Iago's exploitation of Othello's jealousy</u> that leads to <u>Othello's downfall."</u>*

By underlining all of the key information, we can now organise the facts from the above paragraph into something easier to remember:

- *Key theme = jealousy;*

- *Iago warns Othello of "green-eyed monster";*

- *Iago exploits Othello's jealousy;*

- *This results in Othello's downfall.*

This method allows you to organise information succinctly, so when you return to read it later, you can absorb the vital facts and leave everything else out. By limiting yourself to these facts, you can focus on the details which are necessary. This is useful because you don't want to overload your brain with long, clunky sentences when all you need is the important stuff. Your priority should be to transfer the notes into an easily digestible format.

For longer pieces of text with more vital information, you may need to write notes in full sentences. This can be a great way to improve your handwriting and writing skills. The other beneficial part of this method comes in the form of re-writing the information in your own words. It may be tempting to fall into the habit of copying information word-for-word, and you might find yourself doing this without even thinking about it.

If you're doing this, you're probably not internalising the information, and you might not even understand it properly. There are plenty of machines capable of copying things exactly, but that doesn't mean that they understand the information that they're making copies of! So, you should prove that you understand what you're reading by turning it into your own words. For example:

> *"One of the key themes of William Shakespeare's 'Othello' is jealousy. Iago warns Othello of jealousy being a "green-eyed monster," and ultimately it's Iago's exploitation of Othello's jealousy that leads to Othello's downfall."*

This could become:

> *"Jealousy is the main theme of 'Othello'. In the play, Iago warns Othello that jealousy is a "green-eyed monster". In the end, Iago takes advantage of Othello's jealous nature and this results in Othello's downfall."*

Here, the content of both texts remains largely the same. However, by writing the work in your own words, you are demonstrating to yourself that you have identified the key parts of the text and understood them. Writing information in your own words is a great way to test your comprehension of the text; if you're able to sum up the message of the paragraph in your own words, then you probably understand its content quite well.

> Note: Think before underlining or writing in textbooks. If the book doesn't belong to you, it's likely that you won't be allowed to write in it!

Although writing notes allows you to read over them later, the key part of this process is writing them in the first place. When you turn notes from a text into your own writing, you're committing it to memory. Reading it afterwards may be helpful in the short-term, but actually writing it sinks into your head more easily, and it's more likely to become part of your long-term memory.

Visual learners also benefit from making their work more vibrant and striking. This can be done by using different text sizes or colours.

For instance, you could write more important words in larger text so that they stand out more. So, when you return to read your notes, you'll see the vital details immediately.

> "*Jealousy* is the *main theme* of 'Othello'. In the play, *Iago warns Othello* that jealousy is a "*green-eyed monster*". In the end, *Iago takes advantage of Othello's jealous nature* and this results in *Othello's downfall.*"

Different colours could represent different things in your work. For example, if you were given a text including the pros and cons of nuclear energy, you could highlight the positive parts in green and the negative parts in red. Then, you could use a colour such as amber (or orange) to show important details which aren't necessarily positive or negative.

This traffic light system can be used in all sorts of ways. If you were reading a poem for English Literature, you might notice different themes. The main (most important) themes could be highlighted in green, less important themes can be highlighted in amber and then the least important themes could be highlighted in red.

Finally, you can write your notes as tables if it suits the topic. This is particularly useful for making note of 'for and against' parts of your course.

Note-taking is a great technique for any kind of learner to make use of, but it's certainly most beneficial for visual learners. For some people, note-taking is the foundation for all of their revision, and they use other activities to simply break up huge chunks of writing notes over and over. It can certainly be monotonous, but it's a tried-and-tested method that lots of students have made use of.

Note-taking: Pros and Cons

Pros	Cons
Simple and often effective	Can be a strain on the hands after long periods of writing
Doesn't require anything other than a pen, paper, and textbooks	Can be incredibly monotonous
Can be used to practise handwriting as well	
Leaves you with pages of notes that you can read more casually	
Rewriting information shows you understand it better	

Mind Maps

Another great way of visually representing your notes, is by creating mind maps. These are webs of ideas and information connected to each other, to show how they are related. Generally, a central concept appears in the centre of a page, and then other details spread away from it. This is excellent for quickly jotting down all of the information you can remember, and then organising it into sections.

Mind Maps: Pros and Cons

Pros	Cons
Can be made by hand or on a computer	Not effective for some subjects, such as Maths
If done by hand, can be a great way of improving handwriting	Has the potential to be less efficient and more time consuming than other methods such as note-taking

Forces you to write incredibly concise notes, which is great for remembering	Not necessarily an excellent method if you aren't particularly creative
Excellent for subjects with lots of connected events or concepts	
Allows you to be creative which can alleviate some stress	
Excellent for memory since you can visually recall the entire mind map in your head	

Videos, Animations, and Slideshows

Visual learners can benefit greatly from watching videos and animations to help them revise. There's a wealth of videos online, often made by people who recently sat exams, which can be used to help you get a better grasp of the material. Head over to a popular video-sharing website such as YouTube and search for the topic you're currently revising. Always double-check that the information that they give is correct and relevant (by comparing what the videos say to what's in your own textbooks), because it's possible that these people studied a different curriculum to you.

Watching videos created by people who didn't write your textbooks is great for some subjects because it may offer alternative opinions and viewpoints. This is especially useful for essay-based subjects such as English Literature, History, and Religious Studies, where having a range of interpretations and different opinions at your disposal can flesh out your answers even further. This is less important for other subjects such as the sciences or Maths, but nevertheless these videos still serve their function of being interesting to the eye.

Outside of the usual video-sharing sites, there are plenty of online resources which will give you videos, animations and slideshows to help you get your head around whatever you're currently revising. Again, remember to check that the information you're receiving matches what's on your modules.

This method is great for splitting up long sessions of note-taking. If you've spent the whole day revising, and you're getting tired of writing down notes, watching some revision videos online might provide some relief.

Note: watching videos online can be an excellent way of revising, but make sure that you stay on topic. It's far too easy to get distracted by everything else on the internet (e.g. social media, online games) — stay focused!

Visual Aids: Pros and Cons

Pros	Cons
Can be interesting or even funny to watch, and this can help ideas stick in your brain	Access to the internet can lead to easy distractions if you don't exercise self-restraint
Can give you an insight on alternative arguments and points of view	Sometimes the content in the videos won't completely match that of your module – some things might not be relevant
Works as a good break from more intensive revision activities	

Am I a Visual Learner?

Do you find that you can recall information based on how it's displayed on a page? Try taking some notes or making a mind map based on resources in your textbooks, then turn the paper over and try and re-write the notes. Once you've re-written everything, flip the original page back over and see how well you did at remembering it all. If you could remember most or all of it, that probably means that you can learn from visual aids.

Aural Learning

Aural learning is all about listening, both to your own voice and others. Aural learners absorb information by listening to it being said, either by themselves or by others. While it only really involves your ears, aural learning is incredibly flexible. There are plenty of ways to revise effectively if you are an aural learner.

Aural learning is excellent for courses which have lots of short, sweet bits of information. For example, visual learners will likely write the process down as a series of bullet points, or perhaps a flow chart, whilst aural learners will want to listen to each of these points individually, to allow them to sink in.

Reading Out Loud

This is the simplest method of aural learning, and can be done on your own and without any extra equipment. All you need is yourself, your textbook (or other study materials) and your voice!

Start by opening on a chapter or paragraph that you're comfortable with, and then begin to read it to yourself out loud. When you come across a sentence or point which might be more complicated or confusing, read it multiple times. By doing this, it will stick in your head more, making you more likely to remember it.

Aural learners can benefit from using certain tones for different points. Singing notes that you need to remember, or creating catchy rhymes for them, can help you to keep them in mind more easily. It might sound silly at first, but they can be incredibly useful.

Aural learners can create acrostics and mnemonics to help them remember difficult spellings or more complex ideas. Acrostics and mnemonics are almost opposites of one another. An acrostic is a phrase you keep in mind to remember lots of smaller phrases or information.

Mnemonics, on the other hand, are a collection of words used to remember a single, larger word. These are particularly good for spellings:

BECAUSE = **B**ig **E**lephants **C**an't **A**lways **U**se **S**mall **E**xits

The colours in the rainbow can be remembered using the following mnemonic:

ROYGBIV = **R**ichard **O**f **Y**ork **G**ave **B**attle **I**n **V**ain

You can also use this acrostic to help you remember the colours of the rainbow!

Red

Orange

Yellow

Green

Blue

Indigo

Violet

Aural leaners can repeat the phrase "ROYGBIV" or "Richard of York gave battle in vain" until it sinks in fully. Then, if you got stuck in a test, all you'd need to do is recall the phrase!

Of course, the content at the level you're studying at will be much more complicated than "ROYGBIV" or the spelling of "because". However, these exercises can still be used to remember key formulae and phrases.

Note: any kind of learner can make use of acrostics and mnemonics. Even if you aren't an aural learner, try them yourself!

Reading Out Loud: Pros and Cons

Pros	Cons
Requires very little equipment to get started	Requires a specific environment – a place where you're on your own and can speak out loud
Acrostics and other rhymes are bite-sized, meaning you can try remembering them on the go	Can eventually get tiring
Great for making sure you're actually reading the material and taking it in	
Has the potential for self-recording (see below)	

Self-recording

For this technique, all you need is your voice, some reading material and a device which you can record yourself with. In the past, you would have had to use a specific device called a dictation machine to record yourself. Nowadays, almost any smartphone or tablet has voice recording capabilities. So long as it has a microphone, it should be able to record your voice as well. If these options aren't available, dictation machines aren't too expensive, and they might be worth the investment.

> Note: Many laptops can record your voice too. If it has a camera, it's probably capable of recording your voice with its microphone!

If you've chosen to use the "reading aloud" method of revision, you might as well record yourself at the same time. The self-recording technique is quite simple; all you need to do is record yourself reading your notes.

The great thing about this method is that both recording and listening help you to remember information. While you're reading your notes out loud into the microphone, you're going to be committing them to memory, just like you would when reading out loud without recording. Once you're done reading all of them, you can listen to them through speakers or headphones whenever you're studying.

Here are some tips to make your recordings even easier to study from:

- Make sure you're not speaking too close to the microphone, or too far away from it. Do a couple of test runs to make sure your microphone is working properly.

- Speak slowly and clearly, so that you can listen back easily.

- Place emphasis on the more important details in your notes. Try changing your tone of voice for certain key phrases or facts, so that they stick out more.

- When you're done recording, send the files to your phone or smart device so that they're always handy.

- Whenever you have a free 10 minutes or so, you can listen to your notes!

Self-recording: Pros and Cons

Pros	Cons
Has all of the benefits of reading out loud	Requires some kind of recording device, might take a while to set up
Allows you to listen back to your recordings later on	

Podcasts and other Recordings

If you don't like hearing your own voice, or don't have a way to record yourself, there are still plenty of resources that you can listen to. Revision podcasts are easily accessible, and quite often free to download and listen to. There are also plenty of resources on YouTube (such as CareerVidz) and other video-sharing websites, which you can listen to via smartphones, computers and tablets.

Remember to make sure that the revision materials are relevant. Depending on the exam board, the topics that you learn may differ. Before listening to a revision podcast, double check that the topics match those in your textbook or syllabus. If you're unsure of where to start, ask your teacher if they know of any resources that may be relevant.

Like self-recording, revision podcasts and other materials are useful because you can carry them with you at any time, with the help of smartphones and tablets. This means that, wherever you are, you can put a bit of time into listening to them.

Another bonus of these techniques is that they can be far less tiring. Reading out loud from a textbook or writing pages upon pages of notes can get incredibly boring, especially after long sessions. Using revision podcasts can often be a slightly more fun way of learning – so make use of it when you aren't feeling entirely up to more formal revision.

Podcasts and Recordings: Pros and Cons

Pros	Cons
Can be used as a break from doing your own revision	Sometimes exact material in the podcast might not match your curriculum
Can offer alternative ideas and opinions which strengthen your own knowledge	Require some kind of device (e.g. smartphone, tablet, computer or mp3 player) to listen to them
Can be stored on a phone or mp3 player and listened to anywhere	
Often free of charge	

Discussing With Others

Many revision techniques can be quite lonely. Sometimes, it's nice to have a bit of human interaction. Thankfully, aural learners can make use of discussion with a revision partner. This is a great revision method if you have a friend or family member available to help. All this involves is sitting (or standing!) with your revision partner and going through the material with them. There are two different ways in which you could do this:

- **Ask and answer questions.** With this method, your revision partner will hold the textbook in front of themselves for them to read, and then ask questions about the material. It's your job to answer them as accurately as possible. If you get the answer correct, congratulations! Move onto the next one. If you answer incorrectly, your revision partner can steer you in the right direction by revealing a bit more information, such as the first letter of the word, or some related details.

If your revision partner is someone on your course, then you should try and take turns asking and answering questions. By doing this, you're both being exposed to the material and can get things done quickly.

- **Open discussion.** This method involves you and your revision partner speaking freely about the material. If your partner is also studying for an exam, both of you should try to discuss without looking at your textbooks or notes. However, keep the books close-by in case both of you can't remember something, or are unsure of precise details. It's also a good idea to share notes too, so that you can make sure that you've got something correct.

If your revision partner isn't studying for the exam, allow them to have the book open in front of them, but so that you can't see it. Then, just speak to them about the things that you're revising, and they can fact-check you along the way.

Both of these methods are great ways to learn with a partner, and are excellent ways of making sure that your other revision techniques are working. Discussing with a partner is most beneficial later on during revision, when you've already learned lots of information by yourself, and just want to test your ability to remember it.

Note: Thanks to modern phones and internet, you don't even need to sit in the same room as your revision partner in order to revise. There are plenty of communication apps and programs that you can download to your phone, tablet or computer which will let you revise with friends.

Discussing with Others: Pros and Cons

Pros	Cons
It's a fantastic way of remembering information, as well as finding out what you know and where you need to improve	Can be difficult to organise, particularly outside of uni hours
Benefits two people (you and your revision partner)	It's possible to get distracted and chat about irrelevant things
It's a great way for friends and family members to get involved in the revision process	

Am I an Aural Learner?

Aural learners tend to focus on what they are hearing and saying more than what they are seeing and doing. If you think this applies to you, give some of the above styles a try. Aural learning is especially useful for those who struggle to sit down and take notes for longer periods of time, and the above techniques can be used by anyone who wants to mix up their revision.

Kinaesthetic Learning

Kinaesthetic learning is all about *doing*, rather than looking or hearing. Kinaesthetic learners shouldn't limit themselves to sitting in one place and trying to write pages full of notes. Instead, they should be finding more creative and unconventional ways of learning. There's a huge range of techniques for a kinaesthetic learner to tap into!

Since kinaesthetic learning is such a broad field, it can apply to almost any subject and any kind of information. If you think you might be a kinaesthetic learner, give some of the following techniques a try.

Flashcards

With flashcards, you'll want to write down some key notes from your textbooks or other revision materials. Take a large piece of card and cut it up into smaller segments. On one side of each card, write down the word or concept that you need to remember the meaning of. On the other, write down the key facts associated with the word. Here's an example to get you started:

Front	Reverse
Sonnet	A fourteen-line poem which is written in iambic pentameter. Uses specific rhyme scheme. Has a single, focused theme.

Once you've written all of your flashcards, turn them all facing front up and sort them into a deck (like a deck of playing cards). Then, take each card, read out the main word on the front, and then try and recall as many of the key facts as possible. You can do this by reading out loud, or by reading in your head – whichever suits you best.

Once you think you've finished listing them all, flip the card over to see if you missed any details. If you didn't, congratulations! Put the card to one side and save it for later. If you missed anything, take note of it and put the card back at the bottom of the deck. This means that, once you've got through all of the other cards, you can attempt the ones you couldn't completely remember before. One by one, you'll start to eliminate cards from the deck, since you'll remember all of the details for each of them. Once you've completed them all, take a short break before trying again.

Another method for using cards is to stick them around your workspace. Write a note on each piece of card and leave it somewhere in your room where you're likely to see it often. Stick some to your mirror or the edge of a laptop screen, or even place them on the wall or on a bookshelf. You can even leave them around your halls room or house so that whenever you stop to make yourself a snack or go to the toilet, you'll still be revising!

Flash Cards: Pros and Cons

Pros	Cons
A pack of small cards is portable, so flashcards can be used wherever you are	Can take a while to put together (writing on individual cards, etc.)
They're incredibly useful for learning key terms and their meanings	
Writing them in the first place helps commit ideas to memory	

Multitasking

Multitasking simply involves doing another activity whilst doing your ordinary revision. By doing this, you'll start to associate certain facts with the things you do. If you enjoy exercise, try listening to recordings of yourself reading out notes, while going for a run or working out in some other way. If you play video games, stop and test yourself on a question every so often. This probably won't work as a main revision technique, but it's a way to do some light revision on a day off, or once you've finished the bulk of your studying for the evening.

Multitasking: Pros and Cons

Pros	Cons
Bite-sized but effective	Doesn't really work as a main revision technique
Can be done anywhere and at any time	
More light-hearted than intense revision sessions	

Learning Games

For this technique, you're probably going to need access to either the internet or dedicated workbooks. You'll want to find games or other interactive tools which involve *doing* things rather than just reading them. For example, one game might require you to match up key words to their meanings, or key dates to the events which occurred on them. You can actually do this one yourself, in the same way that you made flashcards. Cut up a large piece of paper in separate pieces, and then on half of them write a key word. Then write something related to each key word on all of the other pieces. Shuffle up all of the cards, then try to match them up.

Learning Games: Pros and Cons

Pros	Cons
Entertaining and highly effective for kinaesthetic learners	Online learning games aren't always easy to find
Work as a great break from more intensive revision methods	Creating your own learning games can be time-consuming
Can be an excellent way to revise with others	

Am I a Kinaesthetic Learner?

If you find yourself *doing* things rather than reading or listening, then kinaesthetic learning might be the style for you. You might find that it's much easier for you to do something for yourself, rather than ask someone to explain it to you. You might also find that you work best in unconventional settings: maybe you work better while exercising than sitting at a desk.

Looking Back on Your Earlier Studies

In previous books in this series, we've pointed out that GCSEs and A-Levels are great testing grounds for revision styles and techniques. If you've already studied for exams in the past, you can use this experience to your advantage. While different areas and levels of study will differ greatly in terms of content and difficulty, you can still learn from previous experiences with exams and revision in your life. Consider the following:

* What revision techniques worked best for you in previous exams and assessments? How can you apply them effectively to what you're currently studying?

* What didn't work so well? Is it worth giving it another try?

* What exams went well? Where there any tactics you employed during them that might've helped?

* What exams didn't go so well? What can you learn from your mistakes?

Feel free to experiment with learning styles and revision techniques, but don't be afraid to go back to what suits you best. Sometimes, being in your comfort zone is just what you need in order to perform well.

Final Words About Learning Styles

The techniques explored here are only a few of the many ways you can learn and revise effectively. Start by experimenting with the methods we've listed, but feel free to branch out and try your own ways of revising. Different people think and work differently to one another, and so you need to find your own unique way of learning that works best for you. Remember that, just because you may believe that you have a specific learning style, you don't have to stick to a limited range of techniques. Be creative and give everything a try – it's the only way to truly know what works best for you.

ADDITIONAL LEARNING STYLES
- Four More Types of Learner

In the last chapter, we looked at the three main learning styles. While it's likely you fall into one or more of those categories, it's possible that none of them really apply to you. In this chapter, we're going to discuss four more learning styles, with a description and tips for each.

Physical Learning

This approach, also known as the 'bodily-kinaesthetic' style, involves using your body and sense of touch to help revise. Physical learners tend to be into activities which make use of the whole body, such as sports, exercise, or gardening. Physical learners like to think about things while they do these activities, and often use them as a way of working through their problems. They also like to go straight into the physical, practical parts of learning as soon as possible. This style of learning is quite similar to kinaesthetic learning, with the major difference being that physical learners use their bodies more.

Physical learners can take advantage of their sensitivity to the physical world by using gestures and body motions to remember things. For example, if you need to remember a quote for an essay-based exam, you might learn it better by physically acting it out, creating hand and body motions that stick in your brain. Flashcards can also be incredibly useful for physical learners, especially if you move them around a lot or place them around your workspace.

In addition, physical learners benefit from breathing and relaxation techniques to focus and get in a mindset suitable for revision. Even if you aren't a physical learner, you can probably make use of meditation and relaxation to prepare yourself for revision!

Logical Learning

As the name suggests, logical learners make best use of their brain by engaging in logical and mathematical reasoning. Logical learners are adept at finding patterns in information, and can use them to create mental associations between different facts. In particular, they can easily categorise information, essentially using the 'chunking' method of committing information to memory.

Logical learners tend to work through things in an organised manner. They'll work best under regimented revision schemes, and will likely prefer to categorise everything they need to study. The advantage of this is that they'll get to tick things off as they move through the content. This can be incredibly satisfying. Logical learners might also prefer to place everything in a ranked order.

Logical learners are also great at getting 'behind the scenes' of what they're learning. For example, if they have to revise a mathematical formula, they'll perhaps get the urge to figure out *why* the formula is written in a specific way, taking it apart and learning the theory behind it. This is particularly useful for science and maths-based material, but could be applied to any setting.

While logical learners have a lot of advantages when it comes to revision, they need to avoid getting stuck overanalysing one small detail. They can't get hung up on something that's relatively small in the larger picture of their work. This can take some training, but eventually logical learners can adapt to avoid spending too much time thinking and working on one thing.

Social Learning

Social learners are best suited to communication with others, whether during revision or just in everyday life. Social learners work best in groups or pairs, either discussing their findings directly with one another or collaboratively building revision strategies. Of course, they will absolutely benefit from the "discussing with others" method we discussed in the previous chapter, since they'll be able to communicate their own ideas effectively as well as keenly listen to others.

In addition, social learners tend to be good team players. This can be excellent for assessed group exercises, such as presentations, where candidates are tested on how they work with others as well as their individual input.

Social learners should focus on working at least with one other person. Almost any of the methods listed in the previous chapter can be applied to a cooperative setting. A group or pair of learners could make flashcards together, then test each other in a semi-competitive environment. Social learners can also use role plays to remember events or key concepts, especially if they have a large group of people to work with. Social learners can also get together and create mind maps or do learning games to help them remember the most important facts.

Solitary Learning

The final learning style for this chapter is solitary learning, which is almost the complete opposite of social learning. Solitary learners prefer to study alone, and might find the input of others distracting. Instead, they like to focus on what they think, as opposed to what other people have to say. Revision in a quiet, private space is preferable, or perhaps even necessary.

Since solitary learners work better on their own, they don't have the benefit of talking through ideas and concepts with others. Instead, solitary learners can keep a diary or journal – a space independent of their proper revision notes, where they can write down their own thoughts on a topic.

Combined Learning Styles

As you might have noticed, there's quite a bit of an overlap between these learning styles and those in the last chapter. By all means, mix and match between styles and methods to find what works best for you. In particular, the social/solitary styles work in conjunction with the others, so you might find that you best employ a combination of two or three different styles of learning.

In the next chapter, we're going to look at how to ace your coursework and give you the biggest chance of getting a first.

ACING COURSEWORK

So far, we've looked at how to plan your degree, how to research and study independently, and how to find a learning style which works for you. While all of these are important for performing well in your coursework, we haven't discussed how to deal with coursework itself. So, in this chapter, we'll take a look at what coursework at degree level is like, how to prepare for it, and how to complete it.

Bear in mind that, while most university courses have some kind of coursework during their duration, not all of them will. This means that, depending on your degree, university, and modules, you might not have to do any coursework. However, you might still find some of the information in this chapter useful when doing regular unassessed assignments on a weekly or fortnightly basis.

As previously mentioned, it's likely that you will have to complete coursework at some point during your time at university. In this chapter, we'll discuss how to navigate this form of assessment so you can make your way to a first.

What is University Coursework Like?

If you've been through the UK's education system, it's almost certain that you've had to do coursework at some point. The best way to explain coursework in brief is to compare it to the other kind of assessment: exams.

Coursework differs from exams in a number of ways:

- Coursework assignments usually take place over a longer period of time. An exam is expected to be finished in a few hours, whilst coursework at university usually has a deadline falling weeks or even months in the future;

- Coursework at university often gives you more choice than an exam regarding the topic you'd like to work on. Exams might give you no choice of questions at all, whilst for coursework you might be given a few selected areas to write an assignment on;

- Depending on your subject, you will have to write your coursework to meet specified standards, such as referencing systems, and format. Most exams do not expect you to follow the same rules;

- A lot of exams are 'unseen', in that you don't know exactly what's going to appear in the paper until you begin the exam. For coursework, you usually have time to consider all of the possible topics, research them all, then choose the one you'd like to work on;

- Coursework is often continuous throughout the year, whilst exams tend to be situated at the end of a year.

Coursework at university is also different from school coursework in a few ways. Firstly, school coursework tended to take a long time to complete: you might have had one or two pieces to complete in a single subject for the end of the academic year. In contrast, assignments at university are often handed in at the end of a term, and this means you'll have less time to complete each one. You need to keep this in mind when planning your time.

Additionally, university assignments are held to a much higher standard than those at school. You'll be expected to conduct independent research, using what you've learned in seminars and lectures as a springboard for your own ideas. You'll also usually be required to obey conventions that professional scholars would, such as referencing systems and suitable formatting.

Why Should I Bother?

At school, coursework might have only made up a small proportion of your overall mark. In a lot of cases, controlled assessments contribute to around 20% of one's grade in a subject. For some people, this isn't enough to warrant coursework receiving their full attention. Instead, they direct their efforts towards preparation for exams. We absolutely do not recommend adopting this same approach at university for a number of reasons.

Firstly, assignments throughout the year often contribute to significant portions of modules. In essay-based subjects such as History, English Literature, or Theology, it isn't unusual for coursework to contribute up to half of a module's overall mark – even higher in some cases. This means that you *cannot* afford to slack when it comes to the assignments that you'll be given throughout the year. As mentioned in our chapter on planning your degree, information on how much each piece of coursework is worth should be made clear on department websites.

Another reason why coursework shouldn't be ignored is because it's a great way to secure marks for yourself throughout the year. Think of it this way: when you go into an exam, you don't really know exactly what's going to show up. This means that there's a margin for error – you might simply be unfortunate and get difficult questions. For coursework, this margin of error is often slimmer because you'll have more time to choose a topic, research it, get help from fellow students or staff if necessary, then write your response in your own time. This means that coursework assignments are a way of securing reliable marks, just in case the exam doesn't go so well.

Finally, the things you study for the coursework assignments might also appear in your final exams for the same module. This means that your assignments can be used as a form of practice or even revision. In some cases, it might even be worth looking back at your completed work while doing exam revision.

Types of Assignment

Depending on the course that you're studying, and the modules that you're taking, the type of assignment that you're given may differ. For example, Maths students might have to complete workbooks filled with exercises, whilst a History student will need to write essays on a given topic.

What most students will have in common is that they'll all have to complete a body of written work at some point, whether it's a lab report or a dissertation. Therefore, this chapter will focus on the written stages of coursework. However, some of these tips will apply to any kind of long-form work that you're completing.

Assignment Flowchart

The key to high grades in any assignment is planning. If you can nail a good plan and stick to it with all of your coursework, you can make sure that you cover all bases and increase your likelihood of excellence.

On the following page is a flowchart designed to take you through the step-by-step process of completing an assignment – from the earliest stage of choosing a topic to submitting it and receiving feedback. You might find that some of the steps do not apply to the type of assessment that you're working on. In that case, skip the step and move onto the next one.

Let's take a quick look at each of these steps:

Choose a Topic
This will only apply to you if you've been given a choice of topic to write your assignment about. Essay-based subjects usually have a list of different questions that you can choose from, but this may differ between universities, departments, and modules. If you aren't sure, check the department website, or ask your lecturer or seminar leader.

Other subjects may be more limited in the range of topics you can write your assignment on. If this is the case, you can ignore this step.

Choose and Dissect Exact Question
Once you've chosen a topic, or been given one, you might be given a choice of the exact question. It might be tempting to jump at the question on the topic you most enjoy, but be cautious of the questions themselves. While they might cover the topic that you think you understand really well, they might approach it from an angle that you aren't comfortable with. Carefully examine each question available to you before choosing one.

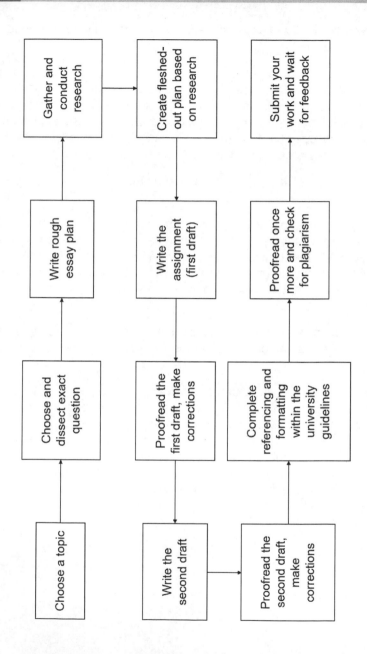

After you've finished choosing a question, you need to take it apart and figure out what it's really asking of you. Keep an eye out for scope, both in terms of the scale of the area itself and how deep it expects you to go.

Write Rough Essay Plan

Once you've chosen your question and know what it's asking of you, it's time to start writing a rough plan. This won't be the final plan that you follow for the entire project – just a loose one to help you gather your thoughts for the research stage.

If you're writing an essay, try to construct a paragraph-by-paragraph plan in this stage. At the very least, you should have a good idea of what the sections of the essay or project are, and how they link together. Once you've finished doing this, you're ready to start the research phase of the essay-writing process!

Gather and Conduct Research

In this stage, you'll spend most of your time reading, working with others, or doing practical work so that you have something to support your assignment with. The exact nature of the research will depend on the subject and module that your assignment is in.

Create a Fleshed-Out Plan Based on Research

Once you've got all of your research together, you now need to apply it to your plan. If you're writing an essay, you want to look for anywhere in your plan where you've made some kind of claim. Add relevant evidence from your sources here so that everything you're going to write in your essay is supported.

If you're doing some other kind of assignment, such as a write-up based on lab work, your entire piece will centre around your research. Again, include evidence from your own research to your plan where relevant so your argument is well-supported.

To make things easier, try to make a note of all the page numbers and locations of everything you're citing in your work. This will save you from having to trawl through all your sources looking for the exact line and page where you got your evidence from.

Write the Assignment (First Draft)

Now that you've got a full and fleshed out plan, it's time to write the first draft. If you've taken your planning seriously, you shouldn't need to refer to any of your sources here – just follow each point of your plan, turning the bullet points and other short notes into full sentences.

If you've already made a full plan, this stage shouldn't take long at all. The key is to follow your plan as much as possible, and turn a series of notes into a coherent, eloquent piece of writing.

Proofread the First Draft

With a first draft finished, you should now read through it at least once. At this stage, keep an eye out for spelling, grammar, and punctuation errors – you don't want your work to contain any amateur mistakes.

Here, you can also get an idea of how your work flows from point to point. If you think some bits don't work properly, or something doesn't fit, make a note of it and then you can find a solution when you write the second draft.

Write the Second Draft

Writing the second draft is less a case of re-writing your whole assignment, but instead looking at the entire piece critically and trying to re-write parts so that they're even more concise. You might feel as though this is unnecessary, but going through and rewording things can help with clarity.

Proofread the Second Draft

As with the first draft, it's important to re-read your work to make sure there are no glaring errors.

Complete Referencing and Formatting

Hopefully, you've been referencing as you go along. If so, there should be little to do in this section when it comes to referencing. Just make sure that you've followed the referencing system that your university and department have specified, such as the Harvard Referencing System. You will probably also need to write a bibliography – do this at this stage.

In addition, you should make sure that the formatting of your work meets the specifications of the department. If your work is word-processed, they might specifically request certain fonts, font sizes, and line spacing. Check the guidelines set by your department since some universities will dock points from assignments that aren't formatted correctly.

Proofread and Check for Plagiarism
In this final stage, you want to proofread your work and specifically check for plagiarism. We'll discuss plagiarism in more detail later in this chapter, but for now ensure that whenever you've used supporting evidence from a source, you've cited them properly. The aim of this is to make sure that you aren't passing off someone else's work as your own.

Once way to check for plagiarism is to copy and paste sections of your own writing into a search engine. If this leads to results of places where you might have gathered ideas from, then you need to cite it as a source or remove the suspicious piece of text from your work. If you do remove It, make sure to replace it with your own work.

Universities take plagiarism very seriously, so it's important that you take extra care when checking for it.

Submit Work and Wait for Feedback
Once you get to this stage, you're basically finished. However, you still need to submit your work. Different universities, departments, and even modules might specify how to hand in your work once it's finished. Some might request a printed copy, whilst others will use an automated system where you can upload your work too. In some cases, they might request both. Your department should make their requirements clear either on their website, or in the introductory documents for the course or module.

Once your work has been submitted, you'll need to wait for it to be marked. Hopefully this won't take too long, but different universities have different standards when it comes to turnaround on assessed work.

When your work and marks are returned to you, spend some time re-reading your assignment to see where you picked up marks, and where you lost them. Hopefully, the examiner has offered some feedback alongside the marked piece of work. Make sure that you read this feedback carefully and take it on board for your next assignment. If you don't get any feedback on your work, or would like more, get in touch with your seminar leader or lecturer.

How To Ace Your Coursework

Now that we've taken a look at the assignment flowchart and touched on each area, let's look at some expert tips for each major stage of the assignment-writing process.

Planning Your Coursework

In many ways, the planning stage of the assignment-writing process is the most important part of submitting an excellent piece of work. If you create a proper plan, then the bulk of the work you need to do will already be finished when you get to the main writing stage.

Treat the planning stage as though you were writing up the actual piece of work, but in a more condensed format. Try to create every point of your argument, with evidence and explanations, and put it inside your plan.

On top of this, divide these into paragraphs and sections, and make a note of ways in which each of them relates to the question and to the previous section. By doing this, you should create a plan that smoothly goes through every major point of your work. An essay or any other kind of written assignment which flows properly will have a much better chance of scoring high marks than one that feels clunky or disjointed.

As we've recommended in the flowchart above, you should try to create two plans for your coursework. The first is a rough plan that outlines the general direction of your argument, as well as some basic points. Once you've done all of your research, you can adapt this plan to create a more fleshed-out one.

Conducting Research

After planning, research is one of the most important parts of writing an assignment. No matter what course you're taking, if you fail to provide evidence for your argument then you will get very few marks. Without conducting thorough research, you won't have the evidence you need in order to create a piece of work that matches university standards.

A lot of the tips we suggested about how to work independently are relevant here. In particular, try to do the following when it comes to gathering information for your coursework:

1. Start by using recommended reading lists provided by the department. This will be a curated list of sources which are relevant to your topic. In addition, they *should* be books, journals, and other types of source which are suited to your level of study.

2. Make use of *reputable* online sources alongside books. By 'reputable', we mean journals and other works that have been formally published/peer reviewed.

3. Unless specified otherwise, try not to use amateur blog posts or online encyclopaedias. If you find a source that you aren't sure about, get in touch with your lecturer or seminar leader.

When it comes to research, you should have a wide range of resources available.

The first port of call should be your university library. Try to get hold of the most essential books from the recommended reading list as soon as possible, since these are the most likely to be taken out by someone else. Once you've got these, read the relevant chapters and take notes on anything that might be useful to your assignment, as well as the page numbers. Get all of the information you need as soon as possible, just in case the book gets recalled and you have to return it.

If you've exhausted all of the relevant materials in the library, get yourself online and see what you can access there. Quite often, universities will give you login details for online journals and journal search engines, giving you access to a wealth of articles and other material that might be useful for your work. Be sure to reference these correctly, since they must be cited in a slightly different way to print journals.

If you don't have access to any of these, some of the sources you need might be accessible in other places. In particular, extremely old works such as Ancient Greek philosophical texts can often be found in their entirety online and free of charge. Of course, more recent works will not be available in this way for copyright reasons.

If this doesn't cover everything, try and find some students on your course in the years above you. If you're lucky, they might have a copy of the book that you need that they could lend to you. If your university has a mentoring network set up between students across years, then this might be a great opportunity to get hold of key materials.

If there are still resources that you need after taking these steps, then you might have to buy the books yourself. When doing this, make sure you buy the correct edition of the book, since different publications of the same book might not be quite as relevant. This is especially the case for translated works, where there might be a large disparity between two separate translations. Reading lists set by departments and modules should include the exact versions you need if this is the case.

Once you have all of the sources you need, it's time to get reading and note-making. When it comes to coursework, it's often better to write out the key information in exact quotes. This is so that you don't exactly re-word something in a way which changes the meaning of the sentence. While you should almost always paraphrase rather than quote directly when writing your assignment, re-writing the quote in full at this stage is preferable. Remember to keep track of page numbers so that referencing is easier later on.

Although most research that students conduct involves reading and taking notes from articles, some courses might require lab work for assignments. In these cases, the work you will need to complete will be set out for you, and you'll likely be given a slot of time to do the lab work. Once you've finished it, you'll probably need to write a report on it. The tips in this chapter will apply to writing a lab report, but be sure to consult documents from your department which might specify conventions and formatting styles.

Once you've gathered all of the research you need, we strongly suggest adding the relevant information to your plan, fleshing it out even more. You might find that the plan you wrote before doesn't quite work in light of what you've learned from research. This isn't a problem: re-write your plan until it suits the kind of argument you want to make.

Writing Your Assignment

Once you've finished planning and researching, it's time to write your piece of work. If you've planned well, this shouldn't be too difficult a task; all you're really doing is turning short bullet points into full sentences. However, there are some tips you can take on board to improve your chances of getting the top grades.

Write the Introduction and Conclusion Last

Sometimes, figuring out a great introduction can be difficult. You want to avoid opening with grandiose, sweeping statements, but you also want to give a general idea of what your argument is. If you've planned properly, you should already know the shape and direction of your argument. However, it's usually better to jump straight into the main body of work. Then, you can write a fully focused and sharp introduction.

Once you've finished writing everything, then you can head back and write a great introduction and conclusion based on what's in the main part of your assignment.

Keep Things Simple

You might be aware of the famous adage from *Hamlet* which states that 'brevity is the soul of wit'. In other words, you should not waste the reader's time; explain points properly, but in as few words as necessary.

In addition, you don't always need to use overly complicated terminology. In some cases, you'll have no choice but to, but in many cases simpler language is preferable. In some subjects, you might be marked specifically on the wealth of your vocabulary and your grasp on language. In these cases, you can be more decadent with your terms.

Another way to keep things simple is to use shorter sentences. The longer a sentence is, the more unwieldy it can become. In turn, this might lead to run-on sentences which are more difficult to read than shorter sentences. Experiment with the length of your sentences to see if making them shorter gives your work more clarity.

Adopt a Good Paragraph Structure

This tip is particularly important for students writing essays. Sometimes, it can be hard to keep a paragraph contained. Students can get carried away with their argument, until suddenly the paragraph contains a lot of complex points.

As a rule, you should try and keep paragraphs limited to one main point. This way, you can stop paragraphs from growing out of control, allowing the reader to understand your argument more easily.

A great way to make your paragraphs easier to follow is to treat each of them as a miniature essay. By this, we mean that each paragraph should have a short sentence which introduces the main point, followed by the point itself. Finally, you should end the paragraph with a short sentence which briefly summarises your point, and demonstrates how it relates to the question that you're answering. This way, you'll have your argument for each paragraph clearly laid out for the reader to see.

If it helps, you can try coming up with a subtitle for each paragraph in your essay. Don't include this in the finished copy, but writing each paragraph with the main point of it explicitly in mind will help you focus your efforts, and create a more consistent piece of work.

Once you have a paragraph structure like this, the flow of your essay will become a lot more pronounced. This means that you'll be able to spot parts that feel disjointed and correct their course. By 'disjointed', we mean parts of the essay which either stick out from the flow of your essay and don't lead to any new points, or sections which actively move against the flow of your essay.

Imagine your essay is a river. Each part of the essay should flow into the next part, as your argument cumulatively builds up towards the conclusion. The points made in earlier paragraphs should always contribute to later ones, and those which don't could be considered as irrelevant.

If paragraphs A, B, C, and D all support a larger argument made in paragraph F, but the argument in paragraph E has no bearing on it, then you need to consider where it's paying off for you. If it isn't benefitting your argument, then you should probably get rid of it and use the space to write something relevant.

There's no set length that a paragraph needs to be, but they can be too long. If you have a single paragraph that's significantly larger than the rest in your essay, it might be worth revisiting it and seeing how to can divide it into smaller parts. This will prevent your essay from becoming 'bogged down'. Likewise, lots of tiny paragraphs can look too fragmented or poorly developed.

Referencing

Referencing is an essential part of most assessed projects. In particular, students studying for essay-based subjects should train themselves to reference sources properly so that their work looks professional and so they also avoid accusations of plagiarism, which will be covered later in this chapter.

Depending on the university, course, and module, the type of referencing system that you'll have to use will differ. Some departments might be more relaxed about which referencing system you use, so long as you make sure that you are consistent. Your department should specify the referencing system that you need to use.

The following are some of the most prominent referencing systems in the academic world, as well as (roughly) which subjects they apply to:

Referencing System	Format	Example	Applicable Subjects	Notes
APA	Author (last name and initials). (Year of publication). *Title of book.* Place of publication: Publication.	Smith, J. (2013). *How to Reference.* London: How2become Ltd.	Social Sciences (e.g. Psychology or Sociology)	
Chicago	Last name, First name. *Title of book.* Place of publication: Publisher, Year of publication.	Smith, John. *How to Reference.* London: How2become Ltd, 2013.	History and Economics	
Harvard	Name of author(s) (last name and initials). (Year of publication). *Title of book.* Place of publication: Publisher.	Smith, J. (2013). *How to Reference.* London: How2become Ltd.	Arts and Humanities	Variant of the APA System
MLA	Last name, First name. *Title of book.* Publisher, Year of Publication.	Smith, John. *How to Reference.* How2become Ltd, 2013.	Arts and Humanities	
Vancouver	Name of authors(s) (last name and initials). *Title of book.* Place of publication: Publisher; Year of publication.	Smith, J. *How to Reference.* London: How2become Ltd; 2013.	Medicine and Science	

Bear in mind that the examples above only demonstrate how to reference a book with a single author. Each referencing system has different formats for each type of work that you're referencing. Here are a few examples:

Edited books	Books with multiple authors	E-Books and pdf documents	Specific chapters of edited books
Newspaper articles	Online newspaper articles	Journals	Online journals
Websites	Blogs	Online publications	YouTube videos
Films	CDs	Lyrics	Religious texts
Acts of Parliament	Press releases	Interviews	Patent documents
Social media	Apps	Podcasts	Maps
Unpublished works	Video games	Archived documents	Annual reports

Each referencing system will have its own rules regarding each of these types of source. Before including one of these sources in your work, find out the exact format.

It's also worth remembering that, when including citations in your work, you will need to cite sources as you go and include them in a bibliography.

The first of these is straightforward. Depending on the rules set by your referencing system or university, you will have to either cite sources *in-text* or by using *footnotes*.

Here's an example of an in-text citation in the Harvard referencing style:

Smith (2013, p. 135) notes that some universities prefer in-text citations.

This citation denotes the year that the book was published, as well as the exact page number it is referring to.

The alternative to the in-text method is to create a footnote. This is essentially the same as the in-text method, except the citation information appears at the bottom of the page:

In his book, Smith notes that other universities and referencing systems prefer the use of footnotes. [1]

The footnotes system is sometimes preferable because it can prevent the text from becoming too cluttered. Most word-processing programs are capable of automating the footnoting system, making it easy to do.

Once you've cited all of your sources in text and written your assignment, you'll need to construct a bibliography. This is a summary of all of the works that you've used when writing your own assignment.

Depending on your university and department, the contents of your bibliography will differ. Some prefer you to include everything that you've read regarding the topic of your assignment, even if you haven't referenced it in your work. Otherwise, they will ask you to only include works that you've referenced. Find out the conventions that your university has set before completing your bibliography.

---

[1] **Smith (2013), p. 136.**

Bibliographies should be filled out in alphabetical order by the surname of the author. So, 'Johnson, S.' would appear before 'Smith, J.'

A final tip for making referencing as easy as possible is to write a bibliography while you're gathering your research. This way, all you'll need to do is copy and paste the same bibliography into your assignment when you're finished with it. This is also a great method for keeping track of what you've read during the research stage, meaning you won't have to trawl back through your notes and books to find exact page numbers.

Proofreading

Proofreading is an essential part of the assignment-writing process for any kind of assessment. Whether you're solving Maths questions, writing an essay, or making a presentation, it's vital that you check for errors. You should look out for the following:

- Spelling, grammar, and punctuation errors;

- Inappropriate vocabulary;

- Unclear points;

- Messy paragraphs and sections;

- Sources without proper referencing;

- Factual errors.

Since this is a lot to keep an eye out for, you should probably do at least two proofreads of your work. On the first proofread, look out for the bigger issues, then move onto smaller errors such as typos in a later proofread, once you're happy with the content.

Another tip for proofreading is to wait for a little while after finishing a draft before reading it. If you start proofreading as soon as you've finished writing, you might be too burnt out to catch the issues. So, once you've finished writing your assignment, leave it for a couple of hours before taking a look at it. This way, you'll be looking at it with a 'fresh' pair of eyes, and you'll be more likely to spot things that need fixing.

Finally, if it's possible, have someone you trust take a look over your work. Even if they aren't an expert in the area you're writing on, they'll be able to tell you if there are spelling, grammar, and punctuation errors. Likewise, they'll probably be able to spot things which are unclear or messy. However, remember to be careful who you show your work to – someone might try to steal your ideas!

Plagiarism

Plagiarism is the act of taking someone else's work and, whether knowingly or unknowingly, try to pass it off as your own. This is an issue that universities take *extremely* seriously, and with good reason. Punishments for plagiarism will vary depending on the severity of the case, but it isn't impossible for them to end in expulsion from the university. For this reason, it's vital that you avoid plagiarism in your work.

As previously mentioned, one of the best ways to avoid plagiarism is to make sure that you correctly cite any information as a source. Think of it this way: if you got the idea from somewhere else, then you need to make that clear in your work. This is why you should make note of everything that you're reading for your assignment – you'll have a record of everything you've learned, and where you got it from.

Of course, it's very unlikely that any idea that you've come up with is completely original. The chances are that, at some point, someone else has thought of the same thing, and they might have even published it. In these cases, you should make use of search engines to look up what you've written, and see if there are reputable sources which support it. If this is the case, then you should cite this source in your work as evidence.

Ultimately, an assignment is about *your* ideas, not everyone else's. While it's important to include evidence for your ideas as much as possible, you must let your own ideas shine through. This might even be through analysing arguments made by other people. However, it's good to err on the side of caution when it comes to avoiding plagiarism.

Some universities have a plagiarism checker built into their submission systems. In particular, universities that use the online submission that we discussed earlier may have a plagiarism checker which automatically compares phrases and sentences in your work to content on the internet. If it finds a match, then you might be penalised for plagiarism.

In some cases, the plagiarism checker might be available to you as well. This can be a good way to spot if there's anything you've cited but forgot to reference properly. However, you shouldn't rely on this – your work should be fully referenced before you submit it.

Self-Plagiarism
Self-plagiarism is quite self-explanatory: it's when you've written something that you've already written in a previous piece of work. While it isn't treated as seriously as the usual type of plagiarism, it's still something that you can lose marks for.

For example, let's say that you wrote a Philosophy essay on utilitarian ethics. If you made the argument that utilitarianism is a poor ethical system because it can't guarantee what the outcome of an action will be, then this would be acceptable. However, if you wrote a very similar point in a piece of work you wrote later in the year – using the same examples, sources, and wording – you'd be at risk of self-plagiarism.

Some universities which use an online submission system will have a plagiarism tracker ready to use. If you've submitted work which is too similar, it could be flagged on the current piece of work that you're submitting. This usually isn't too much of a problem, since you're not likely to be making the same points across pieces of work. However, make sure that you absolutely do not copy from your previous work. In many cases, it probably won't even be relevant.

Submitting Your Work
Once you've finished your work and are happy with it, it's time to submit it. Depending on the university and subject, you might have to submit your work in different ways. Some universities use

online systems, in which you'll need to upload a word-processed document containing your work. Usually, these systems allow for a plagiarism checker either on your own end or on that of the marker.

The other main submission system is the classic physical copy. In some cases, you'll need to supply your department with two copies of your work: one to be marked by the examiner, and the other to be archived for later reference. More and more universities are moving to digital systems because they're often easier to handle and help save paper, but be ready to submit a physical copy of your work if that's what your department requires.

Making Use of Feedback

Once you've got your work back, you'll hopefully have some feedback from the person marking it. One of the biggest mistakes students make when receiving their marked assignment is to check the score and then ignore everything else. Reading the feedback and making sure you incorporate it into your next piece of work is important whether you did well or poorly on the assignment.

If you got a great mark on the assignment, it's important that you know exactly what you did well. Sometimes, the thing that netted you marks might not be what you expected, so it's important to be clear. While you might have performed brilliantly, a good examiner will still try to suggest places where you could improve. Make sure you focus on these areas for your next assignment.

If you didn't do as well as you'd hoped to, you'll likely receive quite a few suggestions as to how you could improve. Take note of these because you'll almost certainly need to act upon them if you want to achieve a better grade next time. Remember that there should still be some areas where you've been given praise – keep an eye out for those for some encouragement that you're getting some things right, and can certainly get better.

Remember that no assignment is perfect, and your examiners don't expect perfection. This is why you should keep an eye on what they suggest improving on, as this will increase your chances of getting a higher mark in your next piece of work.

10 Tips for Getting a First in Your Essays

1. Read the question carefully and make sure that you understand it.

There's only one thing worse than realising you've misunderstood a question halfway through writing you essay, and that's realising you've misunderstood it *after* you get your marks back. Some people like to jump into an essay as soon as they've found a question that they think is interesting. However, by being too eager, students can end up either making more work for themselves when they have to re-write their entire essay, or lose marks because they didn't fully understand the question.

Having a strong understanding of your essay title will help you write the best answer possible. Pay attention to the scope of the question, and look at things such as timeframes. Additionally, make sure that you understand exactly what the question is asking of you. It's never a good idea just to throw everything you know at an essay. Think about what's relevant to the question being asked, then cater your knowledge to it.

2. Take planning seriously.

The best essays come about from meticulous research and planning. Some people spend only a little amount of time on the planning stage of their essay, leaving the bulk of the work for the writing stage. While this may work for some people, what you'll likely find is that you've forgotten something when planning and now have to find a place for it in your essay. This can result in a messy structure, and your essay can lose focus.

The best way to avoid this is to devote more time to the planning stage of your essay. Your plan should be as robust as possible, briefly detailing each section and paragraph. This way, you'll probably end up doing most of the work in the planning stage of the essay-writing process.

Once your plan is finished, and you're happy with the flow of it, then you should start writing the essay. You might find that the actual essay-writing part is easy – all you're doing is turning all of the points you've made in your plan into full-sentences and paragraphs. This also means that you can spot any problems with your essay in the earliest stage, before you've done the bulk of the actual writing. Finally, a strong essay plan will let you know where your argument is going before you've started writing, meaning you can tighten up your ideas rather than just make things up as you go along.

3. Make your essay laser-focused.
Don't *literally* write an essay on lasers. Instead, make sure that your essay is incredibly focused, since this will stop your work from trying to take on too much. Make sure you answer the question, but don't be afraid to take a narrow focus. It's almost always better to go in-depth on a small number of issues, rather than have a shallow analysis of lots of issues. At degree level, your work needs to have depth, so be willing to sacrifice breadth in order to get it.

For example, if a question requires you to use case studies to support your argument, consider looking at just one in more detail, rather than many in brief. This will also help you from going off on a tangent if you force yourself to narrow your focus.

Finally, having a very narrow focus gives you the opportunity to be original in a way that doesn't make sweeping generalisations. A very specific scope gives you the opportunity to go into detail on a minute area, which in turn might give you the chance to say something truly unique.

4. Be concise.
Flowery language and long words aren't always the most appropriate when writing an essay. Of course, you should have some kind of writing style, but this doesn't mean that you need to become incomprehensible. You should aim to make your language easy to understand, with sentence structure that doesn't spiral out of control. As a general rule, short sentences are preferable to longer ones, since you can prevent run-on sentences and a general lack of focus. The goal of an essay is to convey an argument, not to show off with fancy sentence structure. Be sensible and cut through nonsense.

5. Avoid clichés.

One of the most important things to remember when trying to get a first in your next essay is to avoid clichés. This is vital because whoever is marking your work doesn't want to be bored by the same ideas, phrases, and rhetorical devices. For instance, grand-standing is a cliché which detracts from the focus of an essay, and makes it more generic.

Here's an example of grand-standing:

*"Since the **dawn of human civilisation**, scholars have discussed what it means to be human…"*

While this might be the case, it's very unlikely that opening your essay with this phrase will be of any use to your argument. It doesn't shine any light on what you're going to say – all it does is wastes space which could be spent on meaningful discussion. Clichés like this don't come across as confident – it looks clumsy. As we mentioned previously, try and keep your argument to the point, rather than relying on rhetorical devices.

6. Paraphrasing is better than writing quotations.

At school, you might have been taught to quote from sources very frequently. While it's vital that you back up any claim that you make with evidence, a quote often isn't the best way to do so. Let's take a look at why.

When you use a quote as evidence, you'll probably be using it in the following format:

1. Introduce the point you want to make.

2. Give a quote to support the point.

3. Explain what the quote is saying.

4. Explain how this is relevant to your point, as well as the essay question.

When you explain what the quote is saying, you'll probably end up repeating some of the things that have been said. Therefore, you've wasted some space by writing the quote, then putting it in your own words. Instead, you can save space (and look more sophisticated) by ditching quotes and just paraphrasing instead. Not only does this save space, but it also proves that you understand the quote and know what you're talking about.

In some cases, however, it might still be relevant to include the full quote. For example, if you're quoting a line from a Shakespeare play, then the structure of the line, as well as the exact wording, is relevant. So, in these cases, you should opt to provide a quote in its entirety.

7. Make sure your referencing is correct and presentable.

When writing an academic essay, good referencing discipline is vital. Find out what system your university prefers (e.g. Harvard referencing, APA, MLA, Chicago/Turabian) and then stick to it strictly. There are plenty of referencing guides online which will show you to reference every kind of media possible – from written journals to YouTube videos. Go through your entire essay, and make sure that you've cited all of the sources you've used properly. This is an easy way to stop yourself from dropping some marks.

8. Be original.

Originality is a tricky area when it comes to writing an essay. The likelihood is that you're not going to be able to change the world in a single essay. Scholars devote their whole lives and thousands of pages to even the smallest of advances in their own fields. You've probably only got a few weeks and maybe a few thousand words.

Likewise, it probably seems as if all the big ideas have already been made. If you find yourself coming up with a radically new idea when writing an essay, the chances are that someone has already written about it. Being original can be incredibly difficult.

However, if you make your focus in an essay extremely narrow (as previously mentioned), you have a bit more room to work in. In a few thousand words, you aren't going to come up with a whole new theory. However, you might be able to make a small but meaningful difference within a narrow field. Trying to narrow your focus in your next essay in order to show some original thought.

9. Be confident.
Like originality, it's important to show confidence in your essays. After all, an essay is an argument, and the marker wants to see you get behind your ideas, rather than sit on the fence. You don't need to come across as foolhardy or blind to criticism, but don't be afraid to make strong claims if you have evidence to support them.

If you have space and time, try to address possible criticisms of your own argument. You can either address criticisms as you go, or devote a section towards the end of your essay on all the possible issues one might have with your ideas. Awareness of criticisms (as well as the ability to refute them) will show a level of sophistication that will put you far ahead of the competition.

10. Avoid lengthy introductions and conclusions.
Getting started on an essay is possibly the hardest part. Figuring out what you're going to say in the opening sentence can be a stumbling block, and it might be tempted just to start writing mindlessly. However, try to avoid this – you'll most likely ramble on, rather than getting to the point of your argument. Try to save introductions and conclusions for the very end of the writing stage of your essay. Once you know what you've said in the main body of your argument, you'll know what to write in the introduction and conclusion. This will help you to keep these sections laser-focused.

Dissertations
A dissertation is a large project that students tend to take in their final year of university. Not everyone has to complete one, but many students take it since it's the opportunity to sink their teeth into a topic of their choice.

Generally speaking, students work on their dissertation throughout their final year of university, rather than over the course of a few weeks. This is because dissertations are much bigger projects than your usual pieces of coursework. For example, a 'long' dissertation might be twelve-thousand words long, whilst your standard essay might only be three-thousand words. In addition, the level of freedom given to you means that you'll have a lot more independent study to do.

The type of dissertation that you have to complete will differ based on your university and course. Science students will probably have to do at least one experiment, followed by reports based on findings. Humanities students will likely complete an extended essay on a topic of their choice. Since pretty much all dissertations require students to complete a large written task, the tips provided in this chapter will be useful. However, here are a few dissertation-focused pieces of advice for scoring high marks in your dissertation.

Pick an Area That You Find Interesting
When writing a dissertation, you usually have a lot of freedom in what you work on. Since you're going to be spending months on this project, you need to make sure that you've found an area that you find interesting. This might be an offshoot of something you've studied in previous years, or it might be something completely different – often, the choice is yours.

Start Researching as Soon as Possible
While you might have most of the year to complete your project, this time will fly by. If you have your first dissertation meeting at the start of the first term in the year, try to have a question in mind by the end of term. In addition, try to have some books or other sources ready to go so that you can start researching either over the winter break or at the beginning of your second term.

Write Multiple Drafts
We've already suggested this earlier in this chapter, but it couldn't apply more to dissertations. Hopefully, you've been assigned a dissertation supervisor who can read and critique your work. Try and have a first draft ready as soon as possible for them to take a look at, since they'll give you invaluable advice for improving the quality of your project.

Go the Extra Mile
Sometimes, just reading some books and completing the baseline experiments isn't enough to get the highest marks. To improve your

chances, think outside the box in terms of research. For example, there might be an original copy of the main text for your dissertation which is only available in one library in the country. If possible, you could travel there to take a look at it. Or, you might find that there's a relevant scholar doing a talk about the subject that could impact your project – you could attend that. In addition, places such as museums often have archives which aren't readily available to the public, but you can arrange a date to visit and have a look.

Use Everything at Your Disposal

Your dissertation is often such a large part of your degree that it could be the difference between a 2:1 and a first. For this reason, it's vital that you give it everything you've got. Make sure you devote a proportionate amount of time on it (if it's worth a single module, then a single module's worth of time), since it's something that's easily shrugged off until it's too late.

As previously mentioned, you should have a dissertation supervisor who you can meet with a certain number of times in the year. Make sure to meet with them as much as you're allowed to, but always have something of value worth discussing. Here are some things worthy of discussion in supervisor meetings:

- In the early stages of your dissertation, project topic, exact question, and sources are worth discussing;

- In the next meeting, try to bring a minimum of a plan as well as notes that you've gathered;

- In subsequent meetings, try to bring all of the work that you've done on your project, including drafts and notes.

Of course, this is only a rough plan, and you should organise with your own supervisor what you should bring to the next meeting. Whatever the case, make sure that you set these deadlines for yourself as they will help you along the process of completing your dissertation.

Outside of your dissertation supervisor, there may be other members of staff in your department who are relevant to your area of study.

Get in touch with them and, if they're willing, ask some questions which will help your dissertation go to the next level.

Conclusion

Now you should have enough guidance to nail your next piece of coursework. Remember to give yourself plenty of time to complete each assignment that you're given. This will allow you to make the most of the advice we've given you in this chapter.

Once all of your coursework for the year is finished, you'll need to be thinking about revision. This will be the focus of the next chapter.

GETTING STARTED WITH YOUR REVISION

So far, you've had an introduction to different styles of learning, and a detailed look at many revision techniques that can be used in your exams. In this chapter, we'll be shifting the focus slightly, and taking a look at other skills and tricks to help you prepare for any exam. These include:

• How to create a revision timetable;

• How to keep yourself motivated;

• How to prevent yourself from becoming distracted;

• How to avoid cramming;

• How to make use of past papers and mark schemes.

Revision Timetables and Planning

Now that you've had the opportunity to explore the different learning styles, it's time to turn the focus to other general aspects of revision: creating and sticking to a timetable, and making full use of revision materials. Both are extremely valuable when revising, and proper handling of both will improve your grade and make you more likely to score high in exams and in controlled assessments.

The goal of having a revision timetable is to map out all of the work that needs to be done in the time after you've started, up until your exams begin. Your plan doesn't need to be expertly crafted or even particularly nice to look at; it just needs to be clear and easy to read.

The first thing you should do is list every module that you are taking exams in. Once you've done that, try and find every topic within the module.

Do this for every module and for every subject, so that you know roughly how much material there is to cover. It's also worth taking a look at how long each of the chapters for these modules are in your books, or how many lectures were devoted to each, so that you're aware of any abnormally large or small topics.

Once you've done this, it's time to prioritise all of your modules and topics. Some people like to rank all their modules from most important to least important. In other words, it might be worth considering which modules you find more difficult, and giving them higher priority. If you already feel quite confident about a certain part of your studies, place it slightly lower on your list. This means that the areas that need the most attention will receive it.

Once you've prioritised your modules, you can also prioritise topics. Bear in mind that a lot of topics in many subjects are cumulative – which means that a good understanding of earlier topics is vital for getting to grips with later ones. This is especially the case with Maths and Sciences degrees, where you're building up knowledge as you go along. For these ones, it's better to start at the beginning and work your way through, but other subjects might allow you to mix things up a bit.

Your timetable should include all of the material that you need to revise outside of lecture hours. The best way to find out what you need to cover, is to take a look at how your lecturers divide the content, and then use those to fill the timetable. You'll be treated to some blank templates for a timetable at the end of this book. The following example timetable shows what a single week of revision may look like. Look at this timetable to get an idea of how to organise your time:

	Monday	Tuesday	Wednesday	Thursday	Friday	Saturday	Sunday
9:00am–10:00am	**Lecture**		Reading for Seminar		Reading for Seminar	Coursework	
10:00am–11:00am	Reading at Library		Reading for Seminar		Reading for Seminar	Coursework	
11:00am–12:00pm	**Seminar**		Coursework	**Lecture**	Reading for Seminar	Coursework	
12:00pm–1:00pm	**Seminar**	**Lecture**	Coursework			Coursework	
1:00pm–2:00pm							
2:00pm–3:00pm	**Lecture**	Coursework	Coursework	**Lecture**	Coursework	Reading	
3:00pm–4:00pm	Reading for Seminar	Coursework		**Seminar**	Coursework	Reading	
4:00pm–5:00pm	Reading for Seminar	Coursework			**Lecture**	Reading	
5:00pm–6:00pm		Coursework					

Try to make full use of the holidays and reading weeks. These are perfect for getting whole days of revision under your belt, since you won't be in lectures. While you may want to take a break from everything, you should make use of all the free time you have during these breaks. In fact, many students do the bulk of their revision during these periods. Of course, you should take some time off, but make sure you take advantage of 'holidays'. This can really put you ahead for the next term/semester.

How Do I Motivate Myself?

Getting motivated to revise in the first place can be incredibly difficult, and requires a lot of determination and self-control. The earlier you start your revision, the better, but you'll probably be tempted to put off revision: "I'll start next week", or "it's way too early to start revising." Start revising at least six weeks before your first exam. This should give you plenty of time to get through all of your topics.

However, even starting the process can be a pain, and when the exams are so far away it's difficult to get the ball rolling. So, you need to motivate yourself to start revising as early and as well as possible. In this section, we'll take a look at some of the ways you can keep yourself motivated and make sure you get through your revision.

Revision Styles

Start by finding revision styles that you actually enjoy. This might sound ridiculous, but if you can find a few techniques that aren't completely unbearable, you'll be more willing to make a start with revision. Remember that you don't have to be constantly doing 'hard revision' such as note-taking. Mix things up and try a number of styles to keep things fresh early on, then maybe move into something more serious later.

Ease Into It

Before you start, revision can feel like a huge mountain, impossible to climb to the top of. It can be incredibly daunting. You might be overwhelmed by the feeling that you are completely unprepared and don't know enough. That said, you need to make a start sometime. Some revision is better than no revision at all, so if you're struggling to get started with your studies, ease your way into it. Start by revising for a much shorter period of time, and maybe focus on the things that you already know well or most enjoy. Once you're comfortable and confident, move onto something that you're less sure of.

Treat Yourself

Make sure you keep yourself motivated with some treats. You don't need to go overboard, but the "carrot and stick" method of revision can keep you working for longer periods of time, allowing you to get through more work. Things like "I'll get some ice cream, but only after I've done the next 3 pages" are a great way of keeping you going and keeping your spirits up.

Think Ahead

Finally, always think ahead past exams. Life continues after your exams. You might feel that you're not in a great place while revising, that your social life is suffering or your free time is being eaten up by studies, but it will all be worth it when you get great results. This positive outlook – thinking towards the future – is one of the best ways to get you started with revision, and keep you going with it too.

Staying Focused

Sometimes, revision can be a total pain, and you'd rather do anything (even sit around doing absolutely nothing!) than open a book and do some hard learning. It's very tempting to procrastinate, but falling into the trap of putting off revision is one of the biggest mistakes you can possibly make.

Here are our top 5 tips for avoiding procrastination and getting on with your work!

Turn Off Distractions

The first thing you should do before starting a revision session is remove any distractions from your workspace. The biggest offenders for distracting students are games consoles, social media, mobile phones, television, and mischievous housemates. The simple solution to this is to turn off these devices, and put them somewhere out of view or reach, so you aren't tempted to turn them back on and continue texting, messaging or playing games.

Sometimes, however, it isn't practical to move all of these devices. In this case, it's better to find a new workspace, free of electronic devices and other distractions. If there's nowhere in your house or halls that's suitable for studying, the library may be the better choice.

When choosing a place to study, consider the following:

- Is it quiet?

- Are there any gadgets to distract you?

- Will people be walking in and out of the room? Will that distract you?

- Is it comfortable?

- Is there plenty of room for you and all of your notes?

Things get a little trickier when you're using computerised or other online resources such as revision games or podcasts. In these cases, you're going to need your computer, phone or tablet with you, so you'll need to exercise some self-control. Log yourself out of social media if you feel that it's necessary to do so, and make sure to turn off notifications for messaging apps on your phone. You can always take a look during your breaks.

Finally, a few words about listening to music while revising. Be very careful when playing music (especially music with lyrics) while studying. It works for some people, but others will find it incredibly distracting. Experiment with it for yourself, but if you find that it doesn't help you, promptly turn it off.

Give Yourself Plenty of Breaks (but not too many!)

Believe it or not, one of the best ways to avoid procrastination is to take regular breaks. Concentration tends to slide after 45 minutes for a lot of students, so don't push yourself to revise for longer periods of time. If you do this, you'll likely get distracted by almost everything around you, or just get bored or tired. The solution to this problem is to place regular breaks after every chunk of time spent revising.

So, if you revise for 45 minutes, you should give yourself a 10 or 15-minute break afterwards. Start with this and then adjust it as necessary, until you get into a routine which is comfortable for you. Remember not to go overboard with breaks. Make sure that you stick to your timetable and routine, so that a 15-minute break doesn't turn into an hour spent watching TV!

Stick to Your Revision Timetable

Writing and filling in a revision timetable is one thing, but it's another thing entirely to stick to it throughout your entire exam season. If it helps, make your timetable more detailed to include breaks and other activities.

It can be tempting to put off revision or bargain with yourself: "I'll only do 2 hours today but I'll make up for it tomorrow," or "I don't really need to know this stuff, I'll take the rest of the day off." Both of these are risky mind-sets, which don't put you in a great place for succeeding. Good organisation skills come in handy here, and you should try and keep to your timetable as much as possible.

Of course, you can be flexible with your time. Sometimes things come up, and you shouldn't completely sacrifice your social life during the revision period. Just make sure it's reasonable, though.

Make Your Working Environment Comfortable

Outside of keeping things quiet and free from distracting gadgets, you should make sure that your revision space is comfortable enough for you to work in. If the room is too cold or hot, or your chair isn't comfortable to sit on, then you might find yourself not wanting to revise. Make sure your revision space is as comfortable as possible.

Mix Things Up

The final tip for staying focused is to mix things up every so often. One way to do this, is to change the subject that you're revising halfway through the day. This means that you'll still be revising, and you'll keep things fresh. You don't need to switch it up too often, but when you find yourself getting too bored of a topic to continue, finish it and then move onto something else entirely, preferably an area from another subject.

You could also change your revision techniques from time to time, to keep things interesting. If you've spent the whole morning writing notes, why not switch over to a podcast or some online resources? You can refer back to our section on different learning styles to get some ideas on how to make your revision more varied.

Cramming (and How to Avoid it!)

Cramming is the act of trying to stuff in as much revision as possible in the days (or even hours!) just before the exam. It's also possibly the biggest act of sabotage that you can do to yourself.

Cramming happens when a candidate either does very little or no revision before the exams. Before they know it, the exam dates have crept up on them, sending them into a state of panic. These candidates tend to then rush through their textbooks and materials, trying to cover weeks' worth of work in just a few days. In almost every case, this is simply not enough time to adequately revise everything. So, people who cram very rarely benefit from it.

Cramming can actually worsen your performance in an exam. Students who cram often find themselves completely blanking on information when they start answering questions, leaving them helpless during an exam. Cramming doesn't work because you aren't giving your brain enough time to let information sink in.

In an ideal world, you should try to finish your revision for a subject 2 or 3 days before the exam starts. This doesn't always go to plan, but aim to have your revision finished at least 2 days before. Revising the night before an exam is a bad idea, and you should avoid doing so. The day before your exam (and in the hours leading up to it as well) should be spent relaxing and keeping calm, eating well and not allowing yourself to become stressed out by looming thoughts about the test. If you get to the day before your exam and you've finished everything, then you've done an excellent job, and deserve an evening to relax.

Using Mock Exams and Practice Questions

Once you're well into your revision, you'll find that you've got lots of information swimming around in your head. When you feel like you're getting to this point, it may be time to attempt a mock exam. These are excellent ways of testing how much you already know, and it also gives you an insight into what you still need to do in order to ace your exams.

Mock exams are so useful that some people use them and no other techniques when revising. This isn't strictly advised – it's better that you start by revising your notes before trying a mock test, mainly because you may not know enough or remember enough to fully complete a mock exam.

How Do I Find Mock Exams?

Finding mock exams is usually quite easy. The first port of call is your lecturer or seminar tutor, or some other kind of academic advisor. It's possible that they have some mock exams already printed to give to you. If they don't, then it might be worth suggesting that they make some available for yourself and other students.

At most universities, exam papers that students of previous years have taken will be available online or via a local network. Find out where to access them, and get stuck in. However, make sure to check that the module specification has not changed significantly, and that the structure of the exam you will be sitting actually resembles the mock paper! Course tutors and seminar leaders will have all the info you need.

So, while printing pages of past papers can get expensive, it can be a vital way to learn where your strengths lie and where you need to improve. A solution which will allow you to take advantage of mock papers, as well as save you money on printer ink, is to find settings on your printer such as 'draft' or 'ink saver' mode. These will print the past papers out in a slightly lower quality, but usually the papers are still entirely useable.

How Should I Use Mock Exams?

There are two different ways to use mock exams in your revision. The first way is to attempt a full mock exam as you work through topics of the subject. For example, say that you have a Science exam with three different sections. One of these sections is on evolution and adaptation, the next is on the human anatomy, and the final section is about how drugs and other substances can have an effect on the body. You figure out that these are the three topics you need to learn, so you go through past papers online, focusing on questions revolving around these three topics.

Alternatively, you can work through every topic for the exam, and then move onto past papers. The advantage of this method means that you can spend a chunk of time focusing completely on taking notes and using other revision techniques, then move onto working through whole mock papers. This means that you can simulate the experience of being in an actual exam.

Simulating Exam Conditions

Mock papers and past papers are really useful because they allow you to sit a test as if it was the real thing. To do this, find out how much time you would be given to finish the paper in an actual exam – this information can usually be found on the front of the past paper. Then, gather your pens, pencils and other tools, put your notes aside and find a quiet place. Then, get to work with the mock test.

Time yourself with a clock or stopwatch (most mobile phones come equipped with a stopwatch), and see how long it takes you to complete the paper. What's even more useful is to time how long each section, or even each question, takes you to complete. So, if you find yourself running short on time, you know exactly which topics or types of question need greater focus. You don't want to try and speed through your paper too quickly, but if you're taking an unusually long amount of time on shorter questions, then you know that you need to improve on them.

The best part of using mock exams and past papers is that you can put yourself to the test, and make sure of two things. Firstly, you can make sure that you can recall the material you'll need to remember in the real exam. This comes into effect when you simulate a real exam environment, by doing the test under timed conditions and without your notes. While you're doing the mock tests, you'll probably get an idea of what you can and can't recall. Whenever you can't remember the answer to a question, or there's a key fact you can't recall, make a note on a spare sheet of paper, or at the side of your answer booklet. Then, once you finish the paper, you know exactly what you need to go back to and revise some more.

Mock tests are also useful because they highlight things that you thought you knew, but perhaps didn't get entirely correct. This will become clear when you take a look at the mark scheme, which we will cover in more detail later on in this chapter.

After the Past Papers...

Once you're finished with the mock paper, look at the mark scheme and see how well you did. For subjects with clear "right or wrong" answers, such as Maths or the sciences, this is quite easy – all you need to do is read the answer then see if it matches what you wrote. For essay-based subjects such as English, this is trickier since the answers you give aren't necessarily right or wrong. In these exams, you tend to be judged on how well you write rather than what you write exactly. In this case, you might need help from your teacher.

In the next section, we'll examine a mark scheme in more detail. You'll learn how they work, and more importantly how to use them to make your revision more focused. For now, feast your eyes on the flowcharts. These show two different ways of including mock tests in your revision strategy.

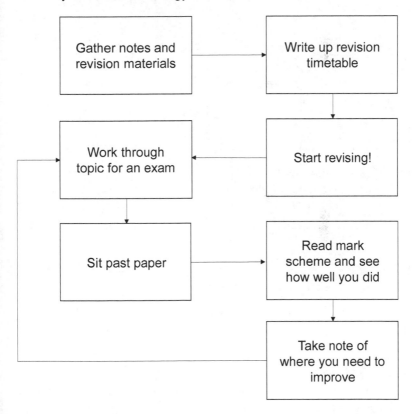

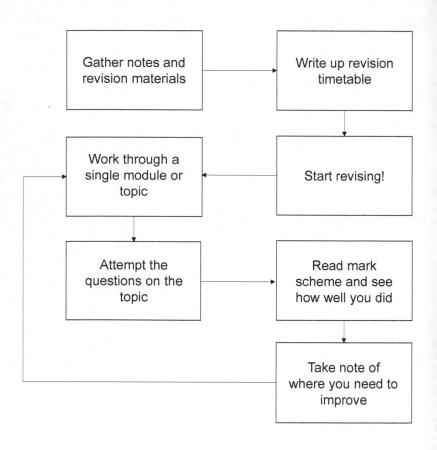

Mark Schemes

Once you've done some practice papers, you'll want to know how well you've done. As mentioned previously, mock papers show you what you need to remember, what you know and what you need to improve on. However, sitting the paper is only half of the story. You'll also need to use a mark scheme to figure out what you do and don't know.

What are Mark Schemes?

Mark schemes are papers which examiners use when marking your exam. In the case of past papers, the mark schemes are the same ones which official examiners would use to mark your exams. So, they're the most accurate source for answers. Depending on the exam, a mark scheme will include different content. For example, Science exams will often simply give the correct answers since the questions are usually either right or wrong.

However, answers to essays in humanities papers aren't as straightforward. For exams with plenty of essay questions, the examiner will have criteria that they will need to look for in order to figure out what the quality of your work is. This is reflected in the mark scheme with a detailed description of what a higher-level essay will look like, and will compare it to other essays of all quality levels. This can make it difficult to mark your own essays – try asking your seminar tutor to give it a look over.

Mark schemes and answer sections can usually be found in the same place where you downloaded the practice papers. Keep away from looking at the mark schemes until you've finished the papers – you don't want to spoil the tests – but have them ready to go.

What are the Benefits of Using Mark Schemes?
Exam Criteria – Essays
Mark schemes have uses beyond simply finding out whether you have the answers right or wrong. In fact, reading mark schemes can be useful even if you aren't sitting a past paper, because they'll show you what type of answers the examiners are looking for. This is especially the case in essay-based exams, such as English Literature, as well as other exams which include essays, such as Languages, and History.

You can use mark schemes to find out what criteria the examiners use to mark your exams, and then compare what you've written to see how well you've done. Have you mentioned the key information that's listed for each answer? Have you answered the questions clearly, using an appropriate structure? Have you checked your spelling? All of these are going to be picked up on in essay-based exams, but it's worth reading a mark scheme to see how much each of these aspects affect your grade.

Exact Breakdown of Marks

Mark schemes can also be used to get an exact breakdown of an answer. Using the same example, the answer may award a single mark for lots of different things. For example, a question in a Biology paper could look like the following:

> *How does an asthma attack reduce airflow?*

One answer given could be:

> *When an asthma attack occurs, airflow is reduced because the following three things happen. Firstly, the muscle walls of the bronchioles tighten and contract, leading to a narrower space. Secondly, more mucus is produced by the bronchioles. Combined, this results in the diameter of the airways decreasing in size. This results in airflow being reduced.*

For this example, let's assume two things. Firstly, let's accept this as an entirely correct answer – it got full marks. Also, let's say that this answer is worth three marks. The mark scheme may distribute the marks as follows:

> *1 mark for mentioning each of the following:*
>
> *Muscle walls of bronchioles contract/tighten;*
>
> *The bronchioles produce more mucus;*
>
> *Diameter of the airways are reduced.*

Now that we know what got us the marks, we can highlight them in the answer written.

> *When an asthma attack occurs, airflow is reduced because the following three things happen. Firstly, the <u>muscle walls of the bronchioles tighten and contract</u>, leading to a narrower space. Secondly, <u>more mucus is produced by the bronchioles</u>. Combined, this results in <u>the diameter of the airways decreasing in size</u>. This results in airflow being reduced.*

So, the breakdown of marks tells you exactly what you need to include in your answer, which will give you an idea of what you need to remember for the exam. Bear in mind that you might need to know more than what's given in the mark schemes, since you could be faced with a question which tackles the same topic but from a slightly different angle.

This information in the mark scheme means you could focus your answer even more. You might notice that a lot of the example answer is not underlined, and these details might not be necessary in order to gain full marks. With the information in the mark scheme, we can simplify and focus our answer:

> *Firstly, the <u>muscle walls of the bronchioles contract</u>. <u>More mucus is produced by the bronchioles</u>. Both of these <u>reduce the diameter of the airways</u>. This results in reduction in airflow.*

Now this answer is much shorter, but should earn you the same amount of marks. So, we now have a much shorter answer, which will give us as many marks as the longer answer would. This saves time, allowing us to move onto other questions in the exam.

'Waffling' is what people tend to do when they aren't sure of how to answer a question. Students who waffle in an exam will add lots of extra words to their answers to fill them out, even if none of what they are saying will earn them marks. We'll discuss waffling in more detail in the next chapter, but remember that reading a mark scheme and finding out exactly what earns you points should help you to avoid writing meaningless rubbish!

Giving Precise Answers

In an exam, you might be tempted to fire off everything you know about a topic all at once. While it's great that you've remembered lots of information, it's not always a good idea to write absolutely everything you know when answering a question. Instead, you should figure out exactly what the question is asking from you. In the above example, we included a lot of information that wasn't necessary to get full marks.

You should aim to be as precise as possible with your answer – get straight to the point in order to save time. Mark schemes are useful here, because they'll show you what the examiners are looking for. You can figure out what's required to get full marks in a question, then focus on giving that as your answer. In an exam, every second is precious; the less time you spend on unnecessary information, the more time you have for harder questions or for double-checking your work at the end. Efficiency is a great skill to have when it comes to exams, and using mark schemes to hone your answers will help you to achieve this.

As well as saving you time, working on giving precise answers can make you sound more confident when giving your answers. Too much information can come across as waffle.

With all this said, it's important that you make sure you answer every question in an exam as fully as possible. If you aren't sure what to write in your answer, it's better to give more information than less.

Conclusion

So, by this point you hopefully have the following: a revision timetable, a comfortable space to work, an idea of what your learning style is, and some ideas to get you started with revision. You've also been given some ideas about how to make use of both mock papers and mark schemes to increase your grade. You're now well on your way to taking your exams and getting that first.

Next, we'll be looking at exams: what they are, how to deal with revising for them, and how to perform well in them!

EXAM TECHNIQUES AND PREPARATION

Exams can be difficult, and you need to prepare for them in two different ways. First, you need to know the content of the exam. This is the actual information that you are going to be tested on – the stuff you've been learning in lessons.

The second thing you need to learn is how to answer exam questions, and how to perform well in exams. This might sound strange, but a significant part of doing well in exams comes down to your familiarity with them, not just how well you know your subjects.

In a later chapter, we'll discuss subject-specific tips for exams. For now, take a look at these general tips, which will help you in the days before and during your exams.

Practise Handwriting Beforehand

If your exams are handwritten, you need to make sure that your handwriting is legible. In the exam room, people tend to write incredibly quickly. As the exam goes on, some students will write more frantically, while others might slowly ease into the exam and get better as time goes on. Either way, ensure that your handwriting is as easy to read as possible.

If the examiner can't read what you've written, they won't be able to mark your work. Generally speaking, it's only the most severe handwriting that results in a significant loss of marks, but if you know that your handwriting isn't as good as it could be, it's worth taking some time to practise it. If possible, try and incorporate handwriting practice into your revision so that you save time. Dedicated handwriting time is good, but you may as well kill two birds with one stone and use revision techniques that help your handwriting, such as making flashcards or writing out pages of notes. If you've been doing mock papers under timed conditions, this should have helped as well.

In the exam, make sure to take your time if you feel as though your handwriting is suffering. If it helps, ditch cursive (joined-up) handwriting so that the words are easier to read.

Finally, you want to practise handwriting so that your muscles are used to writing for extended periods of time. This is important for avoiding hand cramp. Find a way of gripping the pen which is as comfortable as possible, whilst also being able to write efficiently and neatly. Learning some exercises to gently warm up your hands before the exam can also be helpful, and will hopefully make you less worried about your hands giving up halfway through.

If your assessments are based on the computer, you obviously don't need to worry about handwriting. However, if you need to type out your answers, take some time to work on your typing so that you can answer questions quickly and with no typing errors. Being able to touch-type is preferable, but not necessary – just make sure that you can type at a decent pace and with a high level of accuracy.

Come Prepared

Always make sure that you have all of the equipment necessary for completing an exam. This will depend on the subject and the module, so find out beforehand what you're allowed to take in with you.

The following are things that you can take into almost any exam:

- **Black pens.** You should always take a few black ballpoint pens into your exams. You don't want to run out!

- **Pencils.** You might not need these for every exam, but it's worth bringing them for rough planning, just in case.

- **Clear pencil case.** Again, this might not be necessary, but bringing a pencil case can help you be more organised. Make sure it's clear though – if the exam invigilators can't see into the pencil case easily, they may confiscate it because you could be using it to hide notes and cheat!

- **Bottle of water.** We'll talk more about this later on, but bringing a bottle of water can help you concentrate – you don't want to get dehydrated. Remember to make sure that the bottle is clear and has no labels.

Depending on the exam, other pieces of equipment may be appropriate, such as:

- **Calculator.** Certain exams will allow you to bring calculators. Other exams in these subjects might not allow for calculators. If you aren't sure, bring it with you anyway and then leave it under your desk, and hand it to an invigilator if it isn't allowed.

- **Rulers and protractors.** Equipment for solving angles may be allowed for some exams. Like calculators, however, they won't be allowed for others. Make sure that they are transparent (clear).

- **Books.** Be careful with this one. Some exams might allow you to bring in a specific book. Others will be referred to as 'closed-book' exams, which means you can't take in any notes or materials – including the books that you've studied.

If you aren't sure which equipment you're allowed to bring into the exam, ask well in advance.

Keep Calm

Getting a handle on your nerves can be really difficult during exam season, but remember that this is completely normal. If you consider that doing well in your exams is very important, then it would be bizarre for you not to be at least a bit nervous. Millions of people will be going through the same thing as you, and millions more have been in your position and have made it out of the other end in one piece. Life goes on after your exam, even if it doesn't feel like that during the heat of the moment.

Exams are stressful, and the conditions you take them in aren't pleasant either. Being stuck in a silent room for an hour, with nothing but a question paper and your own thoughts, can be incredibly daunting. However, you need to remember that you're not the only one who feels this way, and that a bit of nerves can give you the boost you need in the exam hall.

That being said, you need to keep any anxiety under control. A breakdown just before the exam (or even worse, during it) is uncommon, but just remember that not doing as well as you'd hoped in a single exam isn't the end of the world.

You might feel as though you aren't prepared enough, or perhaps a fellow student has made you unsure about what you've revised – minutes before entering the exam room. This happens often, and can be incredibly demoralising. Remember that how prepared you *think you are* doesn't necessarily represent how well prepared you *actually are*. Sometimes, people who feel poorly prepared for some exams in the minutes before taking it end up doing incredibly well, and some people find themselves doing worse in exams that they felt completely ready for. Essentially, you never truly know how prepared you are.

Besides, what's the use in worrying on the day of the exam? There's no time left to go back and revise some more, so there's no point in getting stressed about it once you're in the room. Try and get into the current moment and power through it.

Here are some other tips for keeping calm in the exam:

- **Breathing exercises.** If you find yourself getting nervous before exams, or struggle to get to sleep due to exam anxiety, then breathing exercises could be beneficial.

- **Get into the moment.** Just before and during your exam, it can help to go into "exam-mode". By this, we mean blocking off outside distractions and any negativity coming from anywhere. Sometimes, having friends and classmates talk about the possible contents of the exam just before entering can put you off. It might make you feel as if you've missed out on something major, and then cause you to worry once you enter the exam room. Put all of this out of your mind as soon as you enter the room. Once you're in the exam, there's no use fretting about those details.

- **Positive thinking**. This might seem obvious, but thinking positively about the exam and what comes after can be extremely helpful. Some people like to change their mind-set about exams, thinking of it as an opportunity to show off their knowledge, rather than as a painful task that they have to work their way through. Alternatively, focus on what you **do** know rather than what you **don't** know, what you **can** do rather than what you **can't** do. Once you're in the exam room, there's no point worrying about your weaknesses. Focus on your strengths.

Read Instructions Carefully

This sounds simple, but far too many people trip up on this simple bit of advice. When you enter your exam, the first thing you should do is read the instructions on the front of the question or answer paper. In some cases, an invigilator may read the instructions to you, but feel free to read the instructions before the exam starts.

Keep an eye out for instructions on what questions to answer. In some exams, you'll have a choice, rather than having to answer every question. In these cases, you need to make sure that you know exactly what's required of you, so that you don't waste time answering questions that you don't need to answer. The only thing worse than finding out at the end of the exam that you answered questions unnecessarily, is realising that you didn't answer enough of them!

When you are given a choice of two or more questions to answer (especially in essay subjects), make sure you clearly show which questions you are answering. In some exams, you'll have to tick a box to show what question you're attempting, whilst others will require you to write the question number in your answer section. Either way, keep an eye on the instructions before going ahead and starting the question. This will prevent you from wasting time answering questions that you don't need to attempt, and also stop you from accidentally missing questions that need answering.

Answer the Easiest Questions First

This tip is absolutely key for the tougher exams you come across, since it's an excellent way to use your time in the exam hall effectively.

Say you're about to sit an exam. You sit down and have the

examination instructions read out to you. The invigilator instructs you to start your exam, and then you begin. You open the question booklet to find that the first question seems almost impossible. Before you panic, take a flick through the booklet and take a look at some of the other questions. If possible, pick the question that looks the easiest to you and start with that.

This is a good technique for two reasons. Firstly, it's a great boost to your confidence when you're feeling unsure about the exam. There's not much worse in an exam than sitting there, becoming more and more demoralised by a question that you don't think you can answer. Starting with more manageable questions will help you ease into the exam, and hopefully you'll recall some information while doing it.

Sometimes, exams can fit together like a puzzle. At first, it seems impossible. But, once you start to put pieces in (answer the questions), the more difficult bits start to make sense. All of a sudden, you're on a roll of answering questions, and then the tough ones don't seem so bad!

The other reason that this is a good technique, is that it represents a good use of your time. There's no point sitting and staring blankly at a question that you can't solve, when there are others that you could be getting on with. Forget about the tough questions for now, bank as many marks you can get with the easier ones, then go back to the hard ones at the end if you have time. This way, you can secure as many marks as possible. In the worst-case scenario, you won't be able to complete the tough questions, but you'll still have earned a few points for all of the others.

Answer the Question

One of the biggest mistakes that students make throughout their academic lives is failing to answer the question that they've actually been asked. This is particularly the case for essay-based exams such as English Literature, but applies to all of your exams.

Focus on Key Details

Some students have a tendency to read a question briefly, then jump straight into their answer without thinking about what's really being asked. For questions which are worth lots of marks, you should take extra care in reading the question fully. If it helps, underline the key parts of the question, so that it's easier to break down:

> *What were the main causes of the First World War?*

This becomes:

> *What were the <u>main causes</u> of the <u>First World War</u>?*

We can figure out a few things from underlining the key points in this question. Firstly, we know that the topic of the question is the First World War. In particular, we need to be looking at the causes of the war. So, our answer is going to be focused on the time period leading up to the start of the First World War in 1914.

However, there's more to the question than this. This question specifies the "main" causes of the First World War. So, we don't need to talk about every single cause of the war, just a few of the most important or biggest things which caused the First World War to happen, such as the assassination of Archduke Franz Ferdinand and rising tensions between the European empires.

<u>Already, we've figured out that we need to answer the question in the following way:</u>

• You need to talk about the causes of the First World War (events up to 1914);

• You need to limit your answer to the main (biggest) causes of the war.

Highlighting the key points of the question has proven useful, because it's pointed out exactly what the question is asking of us. This means that we can save time by answering exactly what we need to, rather than talking about things that won't get us any extra marks.

Don't Twist the Question
Sometimes, students see a question that they don't particularly

like the look of. Perhaps it's for a topic that they've studied well and enjoyed, but the question takes a slightly different direction to one that they're used to. For example, a student may have studied the Shakespeare play *Othello* as part of English Literature, and really liked the dastardly villain, Iago. In the exam, they might come across a question on the play, but not specifically about Iago. The question could be:

> *How does Shakespeare show the relationship between Othello and his wife, Desdemona?*

This question is primarily focused on the main character, Othello, and his wife, Desdemona. While the character of Iago plays into most elements of *Othello*, it might be tricky to include him in a discussion about the relationship between Othello and Desdemona. So, you'd need to avoid straying from the topic of the question, even if there's something you would rather write about. Twisting the question into something that you want to answer is a trap that quite a lot of students fall into, and this ends up costing them marks – particularly in essay subjects. Writing a short plan for your answer, and reading the question carefully, can help you avoid this.

Double-Check the Question

In the next section, we'll be talking about double-checking answers, but it's just as important to double-check the question that you're answering, before you begin to answer it.

Say you're doing a maths question:

> $8.93 \times 9.54 = ?$

Before you start answering the question, take note of everything about it. Where are the decimal points? What operation needs to be performed? Sometimes, people make silly mistakes and misread the question, getting things mixed up.

It's not pleasant finding out that you've answered a question incorrectly just as you get to the end of it, so it pays to look over the question multiple times. In the case of maths questions, it might help to re-write the question in the answer box if there's space. This means you can look back at it quickly, without making any mistakes.

Don't Hedge Your Bets

Hedging your bets happens when a student tries to give 2 or more answers to a single question, trying to cover as many bases as possible and be less likely to lose marks. After all, if you give lots of different answers, surely one of them is bound to be correct? The problem with this is that examiners will mark harshly against answers like these. Take a look at this example of someone who has tried to hedge their bets:

> *Question: What part of the human body carries blood back to the heart?*

> *Answer: Veins/Arteries*

Only one of the given answers can be correct, since one of them sends blood away from the heart and the other brings blood back to it. The correct answer is "veins", but in this example, both possible answers have been put in. This example answer shows that whoever answered the question wasn't sure, so put both down just in case. You can fall into the same trap in longer or even essay responses. Examiners will not award marks for this, so it's essential that you don't try to play it safe in this way. Be confident in your answer.

Avoid Blanking

Have you ever been in a situation where you had something in your head that you were about to say, or about to write, but then completely forgot what it was just before saying or writing it? It can be frustrating in everyday life, but when it happens in an exam it can lead to all kinds of problems. Key details can be forgotten, formulas and tricks may be hard to recall, and sometimes you might just struggle to get off the first page. This is what people refer to as 'blanking'.

Blanking is something that many students worry about, and you've likely heard some horror stories about people who have forgotten everything just as they enter the exam room. However, it doesn't occur as often as you might think, and it doesn't mean you're going to fail your exam.

The best way to prevent blanking is to keep stress to a minimum. This might be easier said than done, but students tend to blank when they haven't had much sleep or have tried to cram their revision into the day before, or the day of the exam itself. This can cause students to panic, and while they're busy worrying, anything that might have been holding in their short-term memory gets forgotten. We'll cover stress in more detail later in this chapter.

In addition to keeping stress to a minimum, make sure that you aren't revising on the day of your exam, and preferably not the night before, either. In order to retain the information in your revision, you need to commit it to what some people call your 'long-term memory'. It takes time for what you've studied to reach this part of your memory, and things revised in the hours before the exam usually haven't made it there. When revision is being held in the short-term memory, you're generally more likely to forget it, which in turn leads to blanking.

If you find that you've blanked in your exam, here are some tips to keep you calm and help you recover from it as quickly as possible:

Take a few deep breaths before continuing. This is important as you need to stay calm. The more you panic, the less likely you are to remember the information you need. Take a moment to calm down – remember that not performing so well on this exam isn't the end of the world, and that you have the entire paper to remember what you need to know and get back on form.

Look through the question booklet. Sometimes, the wording of a question can jog your memory, or give you a clue of what to write. This can get you started on an answer, which in turn can set off a chain-reaction of memories flooding back, to the point where you remember plenty of information. However, this doesn't always happen; don't rely on this as a replacement for revising over a longer period of time.

Start with an easier question. Some questions require less knowledge than others. If you find yourself blanking in the exam, go onto a question that doesn't need as much precise information as others. Sometimes, a question won't be asking for specific terms or details, but rather an analysis or critical take on the material. These are the questions to do first if you find yourself blanking. This won't work for every kind of exam, however.

Don't attempt any of the larger questions. It might be tempting to just throw caution to the wind and get the toughest or biggest question out of the way. This is usually a bad idea, since these questions contain the most marks. You want to answer these once you've remembered as much as possible, so wait until later in the exam to try them.

It's not the end of the world. If you find yourself running out of time, don't panic. Answer as many questions as you can to secure as many marks as possible. It isn't the end of the world if you don't do so well, and you'll have other exams in which to pick up some marks.

Double-Check Your Work

Everyone makes mistakes. It's almost completely unavoidable, even under relaxed conditions, to create a piece of work that's free of any errors at all. In an exam, you're going to feel a bit rushed, and you're probably going to be working very quickly. This is fine, but remember that you're more likely to make mistakes this way. So, it's important that you go back and check everything you've written. Small, silly errors can cost you big marks, so it's vital to make sure you've fixed anything that could be wrong.

Proofreading can take place at two times during your exam. You can either re-read each of your answers individually after you've completed each one, or you can go back at the end of the exam (if you have time) and check every question in one go. There are benefits and drawbacks to both:

Proofread as you go

Pros	Cons
You're more likely to have time to double-check your answers	If you spend too long proofreading, you might not finish the exam
You can take the exam bit by bit	You might be in "exam-mode" and not be as relaxed as at the end of the exam

Proofread at the end

Pros	Cons
You can focus on finishing the exam first before going back to check	If you take too long doing the exam, you might not have time to proofread towards the end
You'll probably be more relaxed once you've answered all the questions	

Both have pros and cons, and one method may just suit you better. You might prefer the methodical approach of checking every answer once you've finished it. Alternatively, you might find it easier to handle the exam, knowing that you've answered every question that you can, and then go back and check everything in one go.

How to go about proofreading your work will depend on the subject that you're taking, and the questions that you've been asked. If you've had to write essays or other longer bits of text, read over your work, checking for errors. Re-read the question, and make sure that you've answered properly. If you haven't done this, quickly add the extra information in the answer box.

If you've missed something out of an essay, the best thing to do is put a little asterisk symbol (*) where you'd like to add more information. Then, in the next available space (even at the end of the essay), put another asterisk, followed by the information that you've missed out on.

When you double-check your work, you might come across something that you've written, but that you know now is incorrect. In this case, you need to cross it out, so that the person marking your exam knows to ignore these incorrect parts. Put a straight, diagonal line through your work, to indicate any work that you don't want the examiner to look at. Then, all you need to do is replace what you've crossed out with something that's correct.

Bring Some Water and Eat Healthily

You are allowed to bring a bottle of water into almost any exam. There may be a couple of exceptions for practical-based exams – such as Art, but aside from that, water is allowed. In fact, bringing a bottle of water to drink in an exam is largely encouraged, because it can help you relax and concentrate.

Some studies show that students who take a bottle of water into their exams and drink it get an average score of 5% higher than students who do not. While this might not actually happen for you, this suggests that having a bottle of water handy can be helpful.

On the same topic, eating healthily (and sensibly!) before your exams can make a big difference. Try and avoid drinking fizzy drinks or eating sweets before an exam. The sugar rush might make you feel on top of the world when the exam starts, but you could have a crash halfway through, leaving you shattered for the final stretch. Instead, try and have a good breakfast in the morning before your exams. See what works best for you, but eggs and fish (such as smoked salmon) can give you plenty of energy to complete your exams with.

In addition to this, some exams may allow you to bring in a small piece of food to eat. Fruit is always a safe bet, including bananas and apples. Basically, you want something that doesn't take too long to eat, but gives you enough of a boost to help you through the exam. Remember to check that you're allowed to take food into your exam before doing so.

Stay Healthy

No matter what happens in your exams, it's important that you stay healthy. This is a slightly more general point, but it can't be emphasised enough.

First, you need to stay mentally healthy. Remember that there's life after your exams, and so you shouldn't put yourself under unnecessary pressure. Some anxiety is unavoidable, but it's important that you don't let it get out of control. Between exams, remember to do things that you enjoy, be it sports, video-games, reading fiction, watching television or spending time with friends or family. This will help you to feel calm during your exam period, and remind you that there's more to life than your exams.

Secondly, you need to think about your physical wellbeing. While you're busy revising and making yourself ready to ace the exams, it's easy to forget about your own health. While it's good to take revision seriously, you can't neglect your own physical needs, and so you should make sure to get a lot of the following during your exam period:

- **Sleep.** Everyone needs sleep in order to function, and you're no different! Adults need between 8 and 10 hours of sleep per night, so aim to get this. A good night's sleep, particularly the night before your exam, can make a world of difference on the day of the test. It will also help you massively during your revision time;

- **A balanced diet.** This is often overlooked, but being fed well can be the key to acing an exam on the day. You want to feel as prepared as possible, so be sure to get a good meal the night before and on the day of your exam. Also, try to eat plenty of fruit and vegetables, since they help strengthen your immune system. Some students work themselves extremely hard, then forget to boost their immunity, leading to colds and flu. You want to avoid this – being ill during an exam is horrible!

Planning and Timing Your Exam

Good planning and timing are two of the most important skills that you can learn and practise before sitting your exams. In fact, being able to plan effectively and get your timing down will serve you well in almost every career, so it pays to put the effort in now.

Before you go into your exam, you should find out exactly what the structure of the exam will be.

Try and find out the answers to the following questions:

- How long do I have for the whole exam?

- What type of questions will be asked (essay, single-word answer, short paragraph, problem solving, mathematical sums)?

- How many marks are there in the whole exam?

- Roughly, how many marks are available per question?

- If applicable, how much time is there for planning?

Once you have this information, you can get to work on applying this to your revision schedule. For example, when you attempt a mock exam, you should try to make the situation as close to the real thing as possible. You should plan and time your mock exam as if it were an actual exam. You can find more about planning and timing your exams in the chapter on subject-specific advice.

Stress

What is Stress?

Stress is an unpleasant sensation that you feel when you're under too much pressure. It's a common feeling to have as a student, especially when studying for and sitting your exams. The pressure that you feel can sometimes grow to become too much to deal with, and can be bad for your physical and mental health, as well as your exam performance.

Stress can be the result of several different worries about your exams. Worries can include:

- Will I get the grades I want/need?

- Have I revised enough?

- Have I left it too late to start revising?

- What will my family and friends think of me if I don't do well?

- What if bad questions show up in my exam?

- What if I oversleep and miss my exam?

- What if I get into the exam hall and forget everything?

Rest assured that, no matter what you're worried about in the run-up to your exams, thousands of other students have felt similar things. It's quite normal to feel a bit stressed during the exam period. However, it's important to keep these pressures in check, and prevent stress from harming you or your chances of acing your exams. The rest of this section will be devoted to discussing stress, and will hopefully give you some advice on how to manage and prevent it.

How Do I Know If I'm Feeling Exam Stress?

It can be difficult to know if you're stressed or not. Some people are genuinely stressed, but dismiss it as normal – perhaps because they do not know any different. If you're feeling stressed at all, it's important to identify it and make steps against it before stress becomes too much to handle.

The symptoms of stress occur because, when the body is under pressure, it releases hormones which trigger 'fight or flight' responses in the body. In prehistoric times, these symptoms may have proven useful for preparing the body to protect itself from a threat, or be able to run away quickly. Nowadays, we aren't particularly worried about fighting or escaping from wild animals, so the symptoms of stress aren't particularly helpful.

Stress has both emotional and physical symptoms. If you have any of the following symptoms, and feel unable to cope, then you might be stressed:

Emotional Symptoms	Physical Symptoms
Low self-esteem	Trouble sleeping
Anxiety	Sweating
Constant worrying	Loss of appetite
Short temper	Loss of concentration
	Headaches
	Dizziness

Whether you think you feel these symptoms or not, keep reading to find some methods for preventing stress, and some ways to reduce the stress that you may already have.

How Can I Prevent Exam Stress?

First of all, remember that exam stress is completely normal for candidates sitting exams. These exams might be very important, and if you're feeling stressed about them it at least shows that you recognise their significance. While stress definitely isn't a good thing, the bright side of it is that you and your body are aware of how important your exams are. Now what's needed is to keep your stress levels down so you can operate at peak performance, and more importantly stay healthy in body and mind!

This section will cover the "dos" and "don'ts" for dealing with exam stress, both during revision and the exams themselves.

DO...

Start revision early. This might seem obvious by now, but starting your revision earlier in the year is one of the best ways to avoid stress. The more time you have, the less you need to do each day. This gives you more free time, and also allows you to make use of extra time to do other revision activities such as practice papers.

Have a countdown to the end of your exams. Buy a calendar and make note of all your exam dates. Tick days off as they go by, and stay focused on the end. Staying aware of the end point of your exams will remind you that there's life after your exams. There is light at the end of the tunnel.

Listen to your body. At times, you might feel like an unstoppable machine, speeding through revision. During this period, it can be tempting to ignore your bodily needs and soldier on. Likewise, when you're worried about not finishing your revision in time for the exam, it seems like a good idea to stay up all night to make up lost time. Whether you're ignoring your body because you're doing well or poorly, it isn't advisable to do so. You can't function properly without food, water and sleep, so remember to take the breaks in your revision to do these things. That way, when you come back to revising, your study sessions will be more valuable because you're able to focus harder.

Forget about the exam once it's over. It's likely that you'll have more than one exam. You might even have multiple exams on consecutive days, or even on the same day. So, it's important not to linger on an exam once you've finished it. As soon as the exam ends, you have permission to forget about it entirely. Try and avoid talking to others about details of the exam, because it might give you second thoughts about what you wrote in yours. There's no use worrying now since there's no way of changing what you've written. Stay confident and move onto the next exam.

Remember that exams aren't the be-all and end-all. As we've already mentioned, life won't end if you don't get top marks in an exam. You might be disappointed by your grade, but remember that life goes on and your exam results won't ruin your life. What's just as important is a confident and prepared attitude, so even if you don't do as well as you'd hoped to, you should focus on moving forward, learning from your mistakes, and enjoying life.

Ask others for support. No person is an island, and everyone occasionally needs someone else to help them through tough times. Exams can be difficult, and a lot of pressure is put on candidates taking exams. When the going gets tough, don't be afraid to talk to your friends and family. Find people you trust and talk to them about your worries. Sometimes, just talking about things can make you feel calmer, even if you don't figure out any solutions. More often than not, your worries will be amplified by the general anxiety surrounding exams, and so talking through your problems and rationalising them can be a form of therapy. You might find that your worries are just the result of paranoia, and aren't grounded in reality.

DON'T...

Rely on online forums. The internet can be an excellent place to find information and techniques for studying. You have access to plenty of specific advice on a range of subjects, and this can supplement your work in the classroom and your revision at home. However, not all resources are useful, and not all environments on the internet are good for your wellbeing. Some exam-focused chatrooms and forums can do more harm than good. You may come across people who are arrogant about the work that they've done, trying to make you feel worse about your studies as a result. Make use of the internet when it comes to your exams, but try not to linger in places that won't make you feel better about your own studies.

Pay attention to how much revision others are doing. You'll likely find classmates who are all too willing to let you know how much revision they're doing, and how well their revision is going. These people are probably having a really hard time with their revision, and are just looking for a way to feel better about themselves. If you need to, ignore these people until your exams are over, and instead spend your free time with people who don't stress you out as much.

Get lazy because your friend has done less revision than you. Just as you'll probably come across someone who's apparently done a lot of revision, you probably have a friend or classmate who has apparently done no revision at all, or very little. While they might be telling the truth, it's also possible that they've actually done quite a lot of revision and they claim to have done little in order to look cool. It's tempting to get lazy about your revision because there's someone else who's done less, but remember that exams aren't about how well others are doing: it's about how well **you** are doing. In turn, this could lead to stress as you realise that you haven't done enough just before the exam. Make sure that you avoid getting lazy with your revision, and this will be far less likely to happen.

Set goals you can't meet. Always remember that there's only so much that you can do each day when it comes to revision. If you've put together a revision timetable then this shouldn't be a problem, but double-check how much work you've allotted for each day. During the revision period, take note of how much you're doing each day, and adjust your timetable based on this. For example, if you're finding that 10 topics is far too many, try reducing it to 7 or 8. Likewise, if you're able to do loads more than 5, experiment and see how many topics you get through in one day. The aim of this is to finish each day satisfied that you did everything you can, and that everything is completed. This should work towards preventing exam stress.

Panic about your exam timetable. Occasionally, you might not meet all of your goals for the day. While this isn't a good thing, you need to remember that you always have the next day to cover what you failed to achieve the day before. At the end of your revision for the day, you should try and put yourself in the mind-set that everything is fine – meaning that you can relax and get some quality sleep.

Rely on caffeine or other stimulants. Caffeine will affect your concentration and sleep-patterns. If you become dependent on it, you'll find yourself unable to perform properly without it, which could lead to uncomfortable and unproductive revision sessions. This could cause stress over time, as you require a certain chemical in your body in order to feel ready to study or sit an exam. In addition, interrupting your sleeping-pattern can make you feel tired during your study time, and can cause stress in general. Do yourself a favour and keep away from the caffeine during the exam period.

Conclusion

Exams of any kind can be incredibly difficult. They can test you in all sorts of ways, and generally ask a lot of you in terms of preparation and commitment. However, this is also what makes them so rewarding when you finally succeed. Exams aren't designed to be cruel, but rather find the right person for the role, or otherwise gauge your ability.

Also, bear in mind that you're not the first person to take exams, and you won't be the last either. This means that there have been years of perfecting exam materials, so you shouldn't be too worried about anything unfair coming to the surface while you're completing them.

If there's absolutely one thing that you must take away from this, it's that exams aren't the be-all and end-all in your life. They're certainly important, and you should take them seriously, but don't let yourself become distraught over worries about exams, or results which weren't as high as you might have hoped. There's much more to life than exams.

CONCLUDING THOUGHTS

So, you now know all the tips we can give you about studying and acing your exams. You've been introduced to several revision techniques, and hopefully had the opportunity to find out what type of learner you are. In addition, you've been given the rundown on exams, and you know how to combat stress. Finally, we've taken a look at human memory – how it works, how to make use of it, and how to improve it to make your revision as effective as possible.

One thing to take away from this book is that exams aren't the most important thing in the world. They might feel like that while you're studying for them, with what feels like a mountain to overcome, but once they're over and you get your results, you should feel satisfied (and proud) of what you've accomplished. Make use of the tips we've provided in this book, try your best, and go away from your exams knowing that you've done something impressive and commendable, no matter the result.

A Few Final Words...

You have reached the end of your guide on how to get a first at university. If you have read the information in this book and made use of the tips provided, you should be on your way to passing your exams comfortably and making yourself proud. Hopefully, you will feel far more confident in what you know as well as where you need to improve.

For any test, it is helpful to consider the following in mind...

The Three 'P's

1. Preparation. Preparation is key to passing any test; you won't be doing yourself any favours by not taking the time to prepare. Many fail their tests because they did not know what to expect or did not know what their own weaknesses were. Take the time to re-read any areas you may have struggled with. By doing this, you will become familiar with how you will perform on the day of the test.

2. Perseverance. If you set your sights on a goal and stick to it, you are more likely to succeed. Obstacles and setbacks are common when trying to achieve something great, and you shouldn't shy away from them. Instead, face the tougher parts of the test, even if you feel defeated. If you need to, take a break from your work to relax and then return with renewed vigour. If you fail the test, take the time to consider why you failed, gather your strength and try again.

3. Performance. How well you perform will be the result of your preparation and perseverance. Remember to relax when taking the test and try not to panic. Believe in your own abilities, practise as much as you can, and motivate yourself constantly. Nothing is gained without hard work and determination, and this applies to how you perform on the day of the test.

Good luck with your university course. We wish you the best of luck in all of your future endeavours!

	Monday	Tuesday	Wednesday	Thursday	Friday	Saturday	Sunday
09:00 - 10:00							
10:00 - 11:00							
11:00 - 12:00							
12:00 - 13:00							
13:00 - 14:00							

	Monday	Tuesday	Wednesday	Thursday	Friday	Saturday	Sunday
14:00 - 15:00							
15:00 - 16:00							
16:00 - 17:00							
17:00 - 18:00							
18:00 - 19:00							

	Monday	Tuesday	Wednesday	Thursday	Friday	Saturday	Sunday
09:00 - 10:00							
10:00 - 11:00							
11:00 - 12:00							
12:00 - 13:00							
13:00 - 14:00							

	Monday	Tuesday	Wednesday	Thursday	Friday	Saturday	Sunday
14:00 - 15:00							
15:00 - 16:00							
16:00 - 17:00							
17:00 - 18:00							
18:00 - 19:00							

	Monday	Tuesday	Wednesday	Thursday	Friday	Saturday	Sunday
09:00 - 10:00							
10:00 - 11:00							
11:00 - 12:00							
12:00 - 13:00							
13:00 - 14:00							

	Monday	Tuesday	Wednesday	Thursday	Friday	Saturday	Sunday
14:00 - 15:00							
15:00 - 16:00							
16:00 - 17:00							
17:00 - 18:00							
18:00 - 19:00							

	Monday	Tuesday	Wednesday	Thursday	Friday	Saturday	Sunday
09:00 - 10:00							
10:00 - 11:00							
11:00 - 12:00							
12:00 - 13:00							
13:00 - 14:00							

	Monday	Tuesday	Wednesday	Thursday	Friday	Saturday	Sunday
14:00 - 15:00							
15:00 - 16:00							
16:00 - 17:00							
17:00 - 18:00							
18:00 - 19:00							

WANT TO IMPROVE YOUR MEMORY AND LEARN EVEN MORE REVISION TRICKS?

CHECK OUT OUR OTHER REVISION GUIDES:

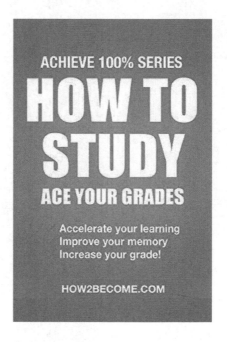

FOR MORE INFORMATION ON OUR REVISION GUIDES, PLEASE CHECK OUT THE FOLLOWING:

WWW.HOW2BECOME.COM

Get Access To

FREE

Psychometric
Tests

www.PsychometricTestsOnline.co.uk